Contents

SO-AWM-543

How To Use This Guide

1. Use the large foldout map to select a tour. Note that each tour route on the map corresponds to the colour of the tour section in the book. The broken lines indicate extended routes without written descriptions.

2. Turn to the section of the book which describes the tour.

3. While you are on your tour, remember to have local tourist information offices stamp your *Stamp Around Alberta* page.

ALBERTA

EDMONTON •

• DRUMHELLER

CALGARY •

MEDICINE HAT •

LETHBRIDGE •

The Kananaskis Tour

Under a stately cottonwood tree in the town of High River, listen to the gentle melody of the clean, cold Highwood River. It beckons you to follow it upstream, to its birthplace in the Rockies. You head west to Longview where again the Highwood calls impatiently, from inside its steep, twisting banks. You are urged on a winding course, west on Highway 541 and north on 40 where Mist Creek and Storm Creek tumble down, uniting to create the Highwood River.

Highway 40 follows Storm Creek to its source near the summit of Highwood Pass, the highest point of paved road in Canada. North of the pass to Highway 1 and Canmore is Kananaskis Country, one of the most unique recreational environments in North America.

The Kananaskis Tour follows the routes of Indians, explorers, fur traders, and cowboys. From vast, horizontal stretches of green prairie fields to monumental vertical thrusts of barren rock, this is a tour of utmost diversity, through Alberta's three major geologic zones: prairies, foothills and mountains.

The diversity of terrain is matched by a diversity of wildlife. The plains and foothills are home to deer, coyote and ground squirrels which co-exist fairly well with human activity. Others, like mountain goat, cougar, lynx and grizzly bear, seek the rugged solitude of the mountain background.

High River

The Kananaskis Tour begins at High River, near the junction of Highway 2A and secondary road 543. High River derived its name from the Highwood River and the Blackfoot word *Ispitzee*. High River was built on one of the few level crossings along the Highwood River. Just north of the present town site, "The Crossing" was frequented by wagon trains, cattle drives and police patrols and, as a result, a stopping house was built. By the late 1800s, the log stopping house was joined by a hotel, a post office, a store and several houses. High River grew slowly and was incorporated as the Town of High River in 1905.

High River still embraces the spirit of the frontier with its Little Britches Rodeo every May and its North American Chuckwagon Races in June. Several High River shops, such as the historic Bradley's Western Wear, carry western wear, locally made souvenirs, and western art. Horsemen across Canada seek the expertise of local tack and saddle craftsmen. Belt buckles by the town's silversmiths are prized around the world as rodeo trophies.

A Walking Tour

The Museum of the Highwood is an authentic

True Western activity spans generations from the Little Britches Rodeo to North American Chuckwagon races.

setting for extensive exhibits of early Canadian trains, as well as Indian, ranching and homesteading displays. Next to the museum the tourist information centre is housed in an old caboose. Here, you can obtain a booklet entitled "Walking Tour of High River." On the tour, you will see the Gateway (Oxford) Hotel which is over 80 years old, and the Charles Clark Residence, built by Charles Clark, Senior, the founder of the High River Times and grandfather of Joseph Clark, who served as Prime Minister of Canada in 1979-80.

An interesting side trip is a tour of Highwood distillers. Pleasant staff will guide you through the distillery process beginning with the cooking of Alberta wheat to the bottling of the spirits. Telephone first for arrangements (652-3202).

In summer, before the coming of the White Man, buffalo congregated on these grasslands by the thousands, and in the winter, Indians found shelter in the river valley. This abundance of buffalo, shelter and water provided all they could desire. There was even a special tree for healing: the Medicine Tree two trees joined by a common branch — was regarded as a spiritual as well as a botanical phenomenon. The Medicine Tree grew old and toppled, but parts of it are displayed at George Lane Park, located along Macleod Trail between Third and Sixth Avenues South West.

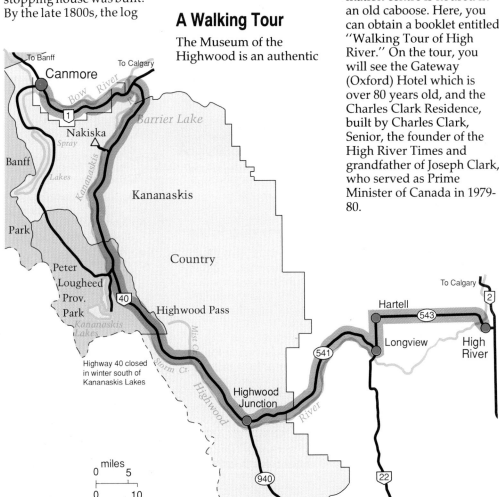

See also the "Walking Tour of High River" booklet.

Scenic lookouts and picnic tables are in abundance along the Highwood River as it leads you to Kananaskis Country.

power of water over millions of years. Its valley was formed by an ancient pre-glacial river that cut a deep, V-shaped furrow in the land. Later, glaciers moved down the river valley, scraping, gouging and bulldozing a deeper, wider, U-shaped valley. After the Ice Age, grasslands flourished and grazing animals moved into valleys and slopes of the Kananaskis area. Indian people followed. One of their major trails followed the Kananaskis and Highwood rivers, making use of the Highwood Pass. Today's Highway 40 incorporates much of this old trail.

Kananaskis Country

Kananaskis Country takes in more than 4,250 square kilometres of mountain terrain including three provincial parks (Peter Lougheed, Bow Valley and Bragg Creek), several life zones and dozens of recreational opportunities.

Like all provincial parks, environmental protection is the guiding philosophy of the three provincial parks in Kananaskis Country. They are managed with an eye to the future, as wilderness areas are a rare and precious resource. Carefully planned development gives the visitor a broad spectrum of activities to be enjoyed in this spectacular setting.

To discover the wealth of things to do in K-Country, stop at the visitor information centre located just inside the park boundary.

West Toward the Mountains

Five kilometres north of High River, take secondary road 543 west across the grasslands towards Hartell, Longview and the mountains.

Why not spend the night on a working farm or ranch? Information on local bed and breakfast accommodation is available at the Longview tourist information office.

Follow Highway 541 as it cuts through some of the most spectacular and historic ranching country in Alberta. Although the era of the great ranches is past, ranching is still a way of life in the Foothills of the Rockies.

On the south side of Highway 541, about six kilometres west of

Longview is the ranch of six-time Canadian champion all-around cowboy, Tommy Bews. Here, Bews operates a working ranch and an international-calibre rodeo school, and gives exhibition rodeos. Group tours and mini exhibition rodeos can be arranged by calling the Bews Ranch (558-2192).

West of Longview is the Rio Alto Ranch, one of the oldest in the area. In 1883, enchanted with the notion of frontier life, Frederick and Walter Ings came west from England after being educated in Spain. They bought a local ranch and named it Rio Alto. They began with only 300 cattle, in a land where drought and harsh weather can destroy half a herd in one year. But they prospered, and now Rio Alto is one of the largest ranches in Southern Alberta. Rio Alto means High River in Spanish.

Highwood Valley

The Highwood River cuts steep banks into the relatively soft limestone bedrock, attesting to the

Agriculture, ranching and oil and gas form the economic base in the foothills.

The Highwood River

The Highwood River has drawn fishermen to its banks for hundreds of years. It is also a popular waterway for rafters and canoeists during the summer, although high water levels during the early part of June may discourage amateurs.

Maps, information and advice are available at the two park information centres, located at both the north and south Highway 40 entrances to Kananaskis.

Plant Life

Take time to discover the variety of plant life in Kananaskis Country.

At higher elevations, white pussytoes and other flowering plants of the subalpine meadows are functional and rather ordinary in appearance. But during two months of the year, they burst into bloom and attract birds and insects, making the most of the short growing season.

Written in the Rock

Travelling the curves and undulations of Highway 40 through K-Country, it is impossible to be unaware of the mountains. They are a record of the personality, power and ancient past of the land. Limestone slabs tell of prehistoric inland seas; sandstone blocks remember broad coastal beaches; and abraded shale valleys bear the scars of glaciation.

Opal Range from Highway 40

There are three stages of mountain development evident in Kananaskis Country: the main ranges straddling the Continental Divide; the Front Ranges through which Highway 40 travels; and the foothills. The main ranges uplifted about 110 million years ago and the foothills about 50 million years ago.

The Rocky Mountains are relatively young and, as a result, thicknesses of rock are exposed, enabling visitors to study the various rock types formed layer upon layer on the bottom of an ancient inland sea. The layers, twisted and faulted in places, are testimony to the powerful movements of the earth's crust that caused the upheaval of the Rockies.

The High Point

At the Highwood Pass, 2,206 metres above sea level (7,304 feet), you are at the highest point of paved road in Canada. Highway 40 through the Highwood Pass is an old route used by Canada's aboriginal people, as they followed game along the Highwood and Kananaskis Rivers. Archaeological digs, made possible by the highway construction, have unearthed artifacts that are 7,000 years old.

Two self-guiding hikes from the summit of the pass provide easy access to alpine settings. The two-kilometre Highwood Meadows Hike is on a raised boardwalk that protects the carpet of fragile alpine vegetation including lichens, sedges and dwarf willows. The five-kilometre Ptarmigan Circle Trail features a spectacular view of neighbouring mountains, a stroll through a 350-year old forest and the possibility of sighting bighorn sheep.

Peter Lougheed Provincial Park

Formerly Kananaskis Provincial Park, this 508 square kilometre park was renamed in 1986 to honour the man who was Alberta's premier from 1971 to 1985. Lougheed was primarily responsible for the development of Kananaskis Country as a multi-use recreational area, financed by an oil and gas revenue savings fund. In provincial parks like Peter Lougheed, recreation is the priority and restrictions exist to protect both recreational and environmental interests. Find out about regulations governing provincial park use at the information centre on Kananaskis Lake Trail. Slide shows, interpretive hands-on displays and knowledgeable staff can guide you to recreational opportunities in the park, and explain the history and geography of Kananaskis Country.

You will notice the Opal Range of the Rockies, on the

The Kananaskis Visitors' Centre provides displays and materials on the geological, natural and human history of Kananaskis.

eastern side of the highway, as you travel north through the park. When earth pressure uplifted the mountains, they folded, faulted and distorted much of the rock layers. On Opal Range, the rock layers were actually turned on edge. The water eroded the softer layers, wearing saw-tooth ridges into the rock.

Wedge Pond Recreation Area

The 8-kilometre long Evan-Thomas bike trail starts here and winds north through shady forest to Kananaskis Golf Course and Kananaskis Village at Ribbon Creek. The picnic area and trout fishing pond are wheelchair accessible.

Campgrounds

You will find the most complete campground accommodation in Kananaskis Country at Mount Kidd RV Park. Mount Kidd features 200 sites with full service hook-ups, a tennis court, sauna, whirlpool, outdoor amphitheatre, grocery store, wading pool, clubhouse and cycling path.

The Highwood Pass offers breathtaking scenery, and interpretive centre and a variety of hiking trails through pine-scented forests.

Kananaskis Country Golf Course off Highway 40. Be sure to book reservations weeks in advance.

Kananaskis Village

The three all-season resort hotels in Kananaskis Village provide a luxury getaway in an idyllic mountain setting. If your budget doesn't stretch that far, enjoy the same panoramic vistas at the nearby Ribbon Creek Hostel.

At an elevation of 1455 metres, experience high altitude golfing at the Kananaskis Country Golf Course, where each stroke carries 10% further than at sea level! The spectacular

Inquire about the "Put and Take" fish program at the information centre.

36-hole golf course features 13,000 metres of diverse and challenging fairway. A river, two streams and several ponds present water hazards, while undulating, irregular-shaped greens, well-placed fairway bunkers, and many trees challenge the best golfers. (You are advised to book reservations well in advance.)

Kananaskis Recreation

There are 95 developed picnic areas in Kananaskis Country, equipped with standard picnic tables, fire pits, firewood, washrooms and terrific scenery.

Every type of watercraft is seen on the lakes and rivers, but swimming is not recommended because the glacial run-off that collects in the lakes is, well . . . glacial. A few kilometres east of the Highway 40/ Trans-Canada Highway junction, the Outdoor Adventure Centre rents kayaks, canoes, river rafts,

sailboards and mountain bikes, so you don't even need your own equipment to enjoy Kananaskis.

You can fish in alpine lakes, streams, rivers and beaver ponds for trout and whitefish. Pick up a license and a copy of the regulations at a fish and wildlife office, a sporting goods store or the Peter Lougheed Visitor Centre. Hunting is allowed only in prescribed areas: information can be obtained at the Visitor Centres and the Ranger Stations.

Kananaskis offers incomparable opportunities for hiking and horseback riding. (Rent horses at Boundary Stables, by the hour or the half-day, or join day and overnight pack trips.)

A leisurely paddle on the Kananaskis River or a white water plunge on the Sheep River. Your choice ....

Kananaskis Country has a variety of hiking trails.

At the designated areas at McLean Creek (near Bragg Creek), motorized bikes and vehicles are permitted off-road.

William Watson Lodge and the surrounding trails are designed as a barrier-free environment, for seniors and the disabled. The picnic sites and trout fishing areas at Wedge Pond and Mount Lorette Ponds are also fully accessible.

Nakiska at Mount Allan

In Cree, Nakiska means "to meet." At the 1988 Winter Olympics, thousand of people from around the world met here to watch international-calibre skiers in action.

This $26 million Olympic facility has perfected runs

Trail riding is one of the most exciting ways to explore Kananaskis Country. However, horses are restricted to certain areas so please consult local regulations.

and state-of-the-art lifts. It has a vertical rise of 918 metres and 70 percent of the runs are for the intermediate skier.

Kananaskis Forest Research Station

As you travel north on Highway 40 past the Mount Lorette Ponds and Barrier Lake picnicking and hiking sites, you'll come to the Kananaskis Forest Experimental Station. It first

Family picnicking at Mount Kidd R.V. Centre.

started as Ozada, a work camp where hungry, desperate men came during the Great Depression to build roads, railways or perform other forms of manual labour in exchange for food. During WW II, Ozada was converted to a German prisoner of war camp, with bright lights, security patrols and high-wire fences. The Colonel's cabin, on site, was the official residence of the camp commander. A memorial display can be seen there. Today, more than 6,000 hectares of this area comprises the laboratory site for University of Calgary environmental and forestry research. A 2.3 km interpretive trail on site provides further information.

Chief Chiniki Restaurant

As you travel north on Highway 40, you come to the junction with the Trans-Canada Highway. Just east on the Morley Indian Reserve, the Chief Chiniki Restaurant offers native Indian food, including buffalo, pheasant, rabbit, venison and trout. The buffalo meat is provided by the Stoney Indian tribe at Morley.

Canmore

A few kilometres further west, in the shadow of the Three Sisters mountain, Canmore is noted for its galleries and shops, as well as its quiet lakes and trails, its mountain climbing school, its adventure tour operators, its nearby guest ranches and its abundance of wildlife.

Winter too has its attractions. Five challenging ski areas are nearby, and annual sled dog races and ice sculpture competitions draw visitors from throughout North America.

The famous Three Sisters is the signature of the alpine village of Canmore.

On the banks of the Bow, near Canmore, the Georgetown Interpretive Trail leads to the site of an abandoned mining town.

Olympic Nordic Centre

Hike the Canmore Trail or drive through town and follow the Smith-Dorrian / Spray Trail to the Olympic Nordic Centre, the site of the 1988 Winter Olympic cross-country skiing and biathlon events. During the

summer, the winding trails provide many opportunities for walking or cycling. The day lodge, cafeteria, lounge and information centre are open all year round.

Memories

Prairies, foothills and mountains are the signatures of Alberta. With the Kananaskis tour, you taste a little of what southern Alberta can offer the traveller. Enjoy new and unique experiences here with your friends and family: it's the kind of country that creates pleasant memories for years to come.

Wildlife

If your eyes are sharp enough, you are almost certain to spot some of the animals that make these mountains their home. If you are not a hiker, watch the fringe of forest that borders the highway. Was that an elk standing stern and still? When you leave the highway for the mountain trails, squirrels, pikas or even bighorn sheep may cross your path, and the air will be filled with the calls of the crows, grey jays, the rat-tat-tats of woodpeckers, and the chattering of the Columbian ground squirrels.

Calgary

Calgary is a city where the impossible tends to happen again and again. As a modest frontier city in 1912, it gave birth to the Calgary Stampede, billed then and now as "the greatest outdoor show on earth." In 1988, barely recovered from a prolonged bust in the oil market, Calgary hosted the '88 Winter Olympics, arguably another of the greatest outdoor shows on earth. What makes this mid-sized city (650,000 pop.) able to perform these amazing organizational and logistical feats is a curious mixture of entrepreneurial zeal, optimism and public spiritedness. Calgarians work hard for their money and, to stage events like the Stampede and the Olympics, they work just as hard as volunteers. When Calgarians make fortunes they have a tradition of giving money back to the city in the form of public bequests and their own time. Buoyed by that kind of civic support, there is little the city of Calgary will not tackle, little that it feels it cannot do.

Visitors to Calgary will soon be struck by the energy and the "think big" mentality of this still-young city. Traffic along the four main highway approaches to Calgary moves swiftly toward the heart of the city and the dominant image is the tall, thick and shining forest of skyscrapers that rises there from the flood plain of the Bow River. When Hollywood's movie-makers went looking for Superman's Metropolis, it was this vista that led them to settle on Calgary as their "city of the future." Entrepreneurial zeal and Alberta's wealth of oil and gas built those office towers but it is the way that the wealth has been channeled back into the city that accounts for Calgary's truly being a city of the future. Construction of sports, cultural and recreational facilities has taken place on a grand scale during the past two decades. The city has also added vast new parks to its already respectable reserves of greenspace. Nor is Calgary all future and no past. Its museums and preserved historical sites show an affection and respect for the city's roots.

There was a time when Calgary was a one-event town. Visitors came to the Stampede or they passed through en route to the mountains. The XVth Winter Olympics showed Calgary to be more than that. It is now a city that rewards the explorer in all seasons, truly a city with something for everyone.

View from the Top

The 190 metre Calgary Tower is located at the very heart of Calgary's downtown (at 9th Avenue South and Centre Street). For a modest price the visitor in need of orientation can ascend by elevator to the tower's observation deck. This truly panoramic view is a chance to see just how Calgary's four quadrants are knitted together.

From the top of the tower, you quickly see that Calgary overlaps a basic change in landscape. Everything west to the Rocky Mountains is high rolling foothills; everything east is prairie, the beginning of the great grass prairie that extends all the way to eastern Manitoba. The Bow River, entering from the west and exiting to the southeast, is the city's broad dividing line from north to south.

If you walk a bit to the right when you leave the elevators, you will soon spot the Olympic Saddledome, home of the NHL's Calgary Flames. Situated southeast of the Tower, it is a silver and red bowl with a saddle-shaped roof. The Saddledome is within the grounds of Stampede Park, the site upon which the Calgary Stampede has been taking place since 1912.

To the right of Stampede Park, looking due south, you will see a round white structure with a roof like a huge fluted seashell. This is the Lindsay Park Aquatic Centre, one of Calgary's many fine sporting facilities. It is open to the public for swimming, running and several court sports. For serious competitors, it has

The Rocky Mountains serve as a backdrop to the city of Calgary.

The Olympic Saddledome has the world's largest free-span concrete roof. It seats 17,000 and is connected to the rapid transit system.

With its uniquely shaped roof, the Lindsay Park Sports Centre complements its neighbour, the Olympic Saddledome.

an Olympic-sized pool and diving towers.

The Elbow River passes in front of the Lindsay Park Aquatic Centre and then winds in behind Stampede Park. If you follow its path from there north to its confluence with the Bow River, you are looking at the birthplace of the City of Calgary. It was this confluence of rivers that led the North-West Mounted Police to choose the spot in 1875 for Fort Calgary. The grassy area that you see between downtown and the juncture of the rivers contains the ruins of that fort: you should be able to see its outline. The park contains the Fort Calgary Interpretive Centre where you can go for a more detailed trip into the history of Fort Calgary and the town that followed it.

Now, look to the right. What do you see? A broad span of railway tracks. Though it is seldom regarded as such, the CPR rail right-of-way is also a historic location in Calgary. By this same route the railway first entered Calgary in 1883 and it brought the settlement era with it. The VIA Rail passenger station is almost directly beneath the tower on the lower level of the Palliser Square shopping centre.

Rafting on the Bow River

If you walk counter-clockwise another quarter turn round the observation deck, you will be facing north. The dominant image on this, the downtown side of the tower, is skyscrapers. As you can see the Calgary Tower is no longer the highest structure in Calgary's downtown. Powered

Notice the sandstone blocks on the old City Hall tower.

by 1970s booms in the Canadian oil industry, the Calgary skyline spurted upward. Despite the levelling off of the oil economy in the 1980s, these office towers are still where decisions are made in the vast Canadian "oil patch." As the oil industry goes, so goes Calgary.

As you move to the west side of the Tower, the eye cannot help but go to the "blue Canadian Rockies" that dramatize the horizon from northwest to southwest. The mountains are an integral part of Calgary. Every weekend the highway west is full of Calgarians going to ski in winter, and to hike, picnic and climb in summer. If you look up the Bow River valley to the west you will see, in the distance, what has taken over as the highest structure in Calgary: the 90 metre ski jump tower at Canada Olympic Park. More about that later.

A Walking Tour of Downtown

The base of the Calgary Tower is a good place to start a walking tour of downtown. Along this walk visitors can see what remains of historic Calgary and many examples of how modern Calgary has been built on the generosity of its citizens. Shoppers will find an amazing concentration of shops and malls.

First stop is the Palliser Hotel, a few steps west of the Tower on 9th Avenue. The Palliser, which celebrated its 75th anniversary in 1989, was the dominant building in Calgary's downtown for decades. In 1914, the year of its birth, the first local discovery of oil (naphtha-rich gas, really) took place in Turner Valley. The strike touched off a stock-trading frenzy in Calgary and many lost their savings to bogus oil companies. Much of this action took place on the avenue in front of the Palliser and a sign in the lobby set out rules for those wishing to drill wells on the premises. The Palliser has recently been restored to its original splendour.

If you cross 9th Avenue and walk east a block and a half, you'll come to the Calgary Convention Centre and Glenbow Museum. The 8-storey museum houses a wealth of art and artifacts most of which were collected by oil entrepreneur Eric Harvie. The new Glenbow building was also constructed with moneys Mr. Harvie left in foundations after his death. Though the emphasis is on

western Canada, you will also find fine collections of European and Japanese armour. The Glenbow has a library and archives dedicated to western Canadian history on the 6th floor.

If you leave the Convention Centre on the south side, you will come out on the Stephen Avenue Mall. The east end of the mall is marked by the new Calgary Municipal Building. This triangular blue-glassed building is worth a look inside and out. On the main floor you can peruse the City Council Chambers and on the southwest corner, you will find the Triangle Gallery, a small gallery where exhibitions of city-owned art, as well as of contemporary works, are

The Glenbow Museum exhibits feature the development of the West, Native people, the building of the Canadian Pacific Railway, oil exploration and a military collection of arms.

staged. On the northwest side of the building, the Old City Hall, a sandstone building with a clock tower, stands in the shadow of its modern counterpart.

The Municipal Plaza directly outside the Municipal Building on its west side, and the Olympic Plaza

The Stephen Avenue Mall in the heart of downtown Calgary includes many old sandstone buildings.

The Olympic Plaza serves as a monument to the volunteer spirit of Calgarians.

The Calgary Centre for Performing Arts houses three prestigious performance spaces.

across the Macleod Trail, together form the heart of Olympic Calgary. Here, tens of thousands of Calgarians and visitors gathered nightly during the XVth Winter Olympics to watch the awarding of the day's medals, to trade pins, to watch the fireworks and light show, and to party and play the night away. It was here that Calgarians showed the world that "Calgary hospitality" is not an empty legend but a living truth about the city.

In summer, Olympic Plaza is a lagoon with fountains; in winter, it is a skating area. For more evidence of the civic support Calgarians give their city, note the bricks that compose the upper, street level of the plaza. On each brick is printed the name of a local person or family who donated twenty dollars to buy that brick, money that went to support the Olympics.

On the south side of the plaza in the Burns Building is the Calgary Tourist Information Centre with its friendly and helpful staff. Immediately south is the Centre for the Performing Arts. The theatres and performing hall in this entertainment complex bear the names of the principal sponsors who helped fund its construction.

Moving west along the Stephen Avenue Mall, stop in at the Alberta Historical Resources Foundation on the northeast corner of the mall's intersection with Centre Street. Here a pamphlet is available which shows you where to look for "old" Stephen Avenue. Calgary was once known as "the Sandstone City" and

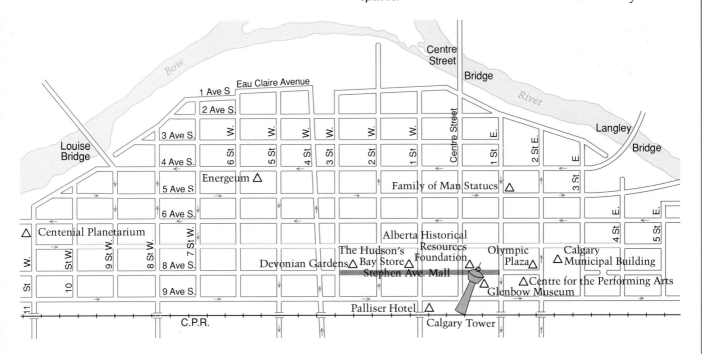

The Devonian Gardens is a unique garden enclosed by glass in downtown Calgary.

Calgary's entrepreneurial spirit has attracted people from all over the world. The skyscrapers accentuate the business atmosphere of the city.

several handsome vestiges of that era can be located with the help of the guide. A block farther west, you come to The Bay with its mosaic-floored colonnade along the east and south sides. From the Bay on, you enter a series of inter-connected shopping centres. You can continue down the outside mall, entering from there; or, if the weather is not to your liking, you can make the journey via the "Plus 15" system. Each of the malls is connected by a second storey system of enclosed walkways.

A highlight on this stretch of your walk is the Devonian Gardens, a 1-hectare fully-enclosed park found 14 metres above street level at the top of the Toronto Dominion Square shopping centre. The park is a biological garden enclosed by glass, complete with waterfalls and quiet lagoons. How did it come to be? The park is another product of Eric Harvie's civic generosity as the park was created with funds from another Harvie family foundation.

The C-Train or LRT, Calgary's fast transit system, is free for all stops along 7th Avenue downtown. You might use it to reach a couple of attractions at more distant locations. The Energeum, found on the main floor of the Energy Resources Conservation Board building at 640-5th Avenue SW, is a museum and hands-on educational centre devoted to an understanding of energy and energy industries. A block beyond the western downtown terminus of the C-Train is the Alberta Science Centre and Centennial Planetarium where you can go for an excellent tour of the heavens. Laser exhibits, holograms and optical illusions are some of the other interesting displays.

Side Trips in the Downtown Area

Within and close by downtown are several more interesting spots. In a park along 1st St. East between 4th and 5th Avenues South, a circle of giant human figures appear to dance on the grass. This is the "Family of Man," first displayed in the British Pavilion of Expo '67. The Family was donated to Calgary by a local construction company.

South of downtown, within a half-block of one another at 14th Avenue and 6th St. SW, are the Lougheed Mansion and the Ranchmen's Club. Respectively, here is the former home of one of Alberta's best known families and Calgary's most exclusive private club. The Ranchmen's is a hold-over from the days when a very British ranching aristocracy ruled over the open range cattle industry. Among those who passed through its marquéed doorway was former member, Edward, Prince of Wales. Edward owned the EP Ranch south of the town of Longview.

East of downtown along 9th Avenue are several interesting sites. The Fort Calgary site and interpretive centre come first and then, just across the bridge, the Deane House, home of

The Family of Man, from Expo 67, is located on First Street East.

North-West Mounted Police drill the tourists at the Calgary Interpretive Site.

The Inglewood Bird Sanctuary sets aside twenty-eight hectares for the observation and study of birds.

an early North-West Mounted Police superintendent. Now restored, the house operates as a tea room and offers tours.

Farther east along 9th Avenue, visitors enter old Calgary of a different kind, a stretch of second-hand stores and turn-of-the-century hotels and schools. Here one can see what Calgary used to look like before '60s and '70s prosperity set in.

Also, from this point the

visitor is within striking distance (a short cab ride) of the Inglewood Bird Sanctuary, 28 hectares of riverside property where a variety of bird life, particularly waterfowl, spend part of their year. Over 200 species have been sighted here. Free tours are available.

Close by, the Sam Livingstone Fish Hatchery spawns 8.6 million fish per year for the stocking of Alberta rivers and lakes.

On the C-Train

Calgary's fast-transit C-train or LRT has made a big difference in the ease with which visitors can take in more distant city attractions: theme parks, sports facilities, educational institutions and shopping malls. Children under six ride free. Your C-Train ticket can be used as a transfer onto Calgary Transit buses.

North on the C-Train

Trains on the northwest leg of the system are marked "University." This could be described as the educational and sports leg of the system. After leaving downtown, the train loops over the Bow River and the first stop beyond the river is the Sunnyside station. This old residential area has in recent years become an important shopping and nightlife area. Fine boutiques and restaurants cluster around the intersection of 10th Street and Kensington Avenue. The train then climbs the hill and stops at the S.A.I.T./Alberta College of Art/Jubilee station. This stop gives you quick access to

Located at the University of Calgary, the Olympic Oval is one of the world's finest speed skating facilities.

the Southern Alberta Institute of Technology, the Alberta College of Art and the Jubilee Auditorium. Two stops farther on, the

Banff Trail station is your access point for McMahon Stadium and Foothills Stadium (homes of the CFL Stampeders and the Triple "A" Cannons, respectively). The last stop on the University route brings you to the University of Calgary. Two of many items of interest here are the Olympic Oval and the Nickle Arts Museum. The Olympic Oval, a fully enclosed speed skating oval, was the venue for that sport at the '88 Winter Olympics. The Nickle Arts Museum houses a permanent exhibition of ancient coins as well as current exhibitions of art.

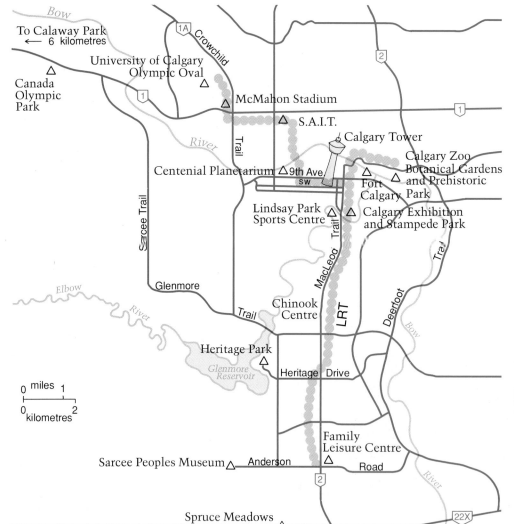

McMahon Stadium

Kensington area

East on the C-Train

Trains on the northeast leg of the LRT are marked "Whitehorn." The Zoo station, the second station beyond the Bow, is your access to the Calgary Zoo, Prehistoric Park and Botanical Gardens. Situated

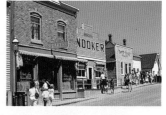

Heritage Park is Canada's largest historical village. Steam trains, street cars, a sternwheeler and vintage vehicles are featured in the midst of a bustling turn-of-the-century town and farming community.

The conservatory is a major section of the Calgary Zoo which serves as an aviary as well as an indoor garden.

One of the fourteen hundred animals at the Calgary Zoo and Prehistoric Park.

on a group of islands in the Bow River, this is one of North America's most respected zoos: respected for its habitat-like enclosures and for its dedication to world wildlife preservation. The prehistoric park (summer months only) is a paradise for dinosaur-loving children.

South on the C-Train

The southern ("Anderson") leg of the C-train is a near instant way of getting to Stampede Park and the Olympic Saddledome. The Stampede and Erlton stations deliver you to the north and south ends of the park, respectively. Stampede Park is most famous for being home to the annual Calgary Stampede, but it is an attraction in all seasons. Thoroughbred and sulky race meets alternate through the year in front of the grandstand. Calgary Flames hockey games and Calgary '88s professional basketball encounters go at the Olympic Saddledome (as do major rock concerts). In the Round-up Centre,

you will find the Grain Academy, an exhibition dedicated to grain farming. Operational railway and elevator models help visitors understand the Canadian farming economy.

Beyond Stampede Park the LRT plunges under Cemetery Hill and, after it emerges, the second station is Chinook. A short bus ride or a ten-minute walk will bring you to Chinook Shopping Centre, oldest and largest of the Calgary malls. The parking area at Chinook is also the site of Calgary's oldest and largest Stampede Breakfast. These free breakfasts, served frontier-style off the backs of chuckwagons, are

another Calgary Stampede institution.

The next station south, Heritage, is your point of departure for Heritage Park. (If you transfer to either bus #80 or #20, it will bring you within two blocks of the park gate.) Heritage Park is a remarkable historical park on the banks of the Glenmore Reservoir. Historic commercial enterprises and houses were brought here from all over southern Alberta and assembled into a frontier town. In the summer months, the blacksmith forges horseshoes, the bakery turns out sourdough bread, the pool hall is open for a game on huge slate tables, the hotel serves meals, the stores sell goods. A steam train takes visitors for rides around the park and the SS Moyie paddle-steamer will take you for a turn around the reservoir. This is only a foretaste of the many delights of this fine park. A highlight of the 25th anniversary of Heritage Park in 1989 is the opening of an authentic antique midway.

Twenty-seven life size dinosaur models reside in the park.

The Wilderness Within

Calgary is known to many who have not visited here as a business beehive, a dense cluster of skyscrapers surrounded by sprawling suburbs. What this generalization neglects to mention is that Calgary has more park space per capita than any city in North America. For the pleasure walker, the serious hiker, the cyclist, the jogger, the cross-country skier and the naturalist, Calgary abounds in green space and natural pathways.

The gardened and groomed Victorian garden-style park is best exemplified by two venerable green areas close to downtown. Directly below the Alberta College of Art off 10th St. NW is Riley Park with its busy weekend cricket pitch. South of downtown, at 12th Avenue and 2nd St. SW, you will find Central Memorial Park. This park, Calgary's oldest, is dedicated to three wars: the Boer War, the Great War and the Second World War,

with monuments to each. The Boer War memorial is the park's centrepiece: an unknown cavalryman on his mount.

The Bow and Elbow Rivers are dotted with fine parks which help both of those valleys retain their natural image. Bowness Park with its large lagoon (free skating in winter) is a Bow River valley park at the far western edge of the city. Trolley rides to this park were a Sunday tradition in the early years of the century. Between

For generations, Calgarians have been drawn to the quietness of Calgary's parks.

Bowness Park and downtown, on the south bank of the river, is Edworthy Park. Its shadowed cliffs have grown up thick in a mixture of deciduous and conifer forest.

Along the Elbow River, from the Glenmore Reservoir southwest to the

A number of Calgary parks, such as Bowness Park featured here, encourage canoeing and paddle boating.

confluence of the Bow, the parks are intimate and close enough together to make for fine riverside hiking or cycling. Starting at the reservoir, the parks are Glenmore, Sandy Beach, Riverside, Stanley, Roxborough, and Lindsay — which brings you back to Stampede Park.

Calgary also has two vast wilderness areas in which you can easily forget that you're anywhere near a major city. The Weazlehead wilderness area adjoins Glenmore Park at the head of the Glenmore Reservoir. The spot where the river winds and fans into the reservoir is extensively dammed by a busy beaver population. A bicycle and hiking route (asphalt path) crosses the Weazlehead and entirely circles the reservoir (7 kilometres). In winter, there is some challenging cross-country skiing along the northern cliffs of the valley.

Fish Creek Park is simply massive. It extends almost entirely across the city from west to east (south of Anderson Road and Canyon Meadows Road). On the far eastern flank of the park, off Bow Bottom Trail, you will find the Bow Valley Ranch and Roper Hull Ranch House. The ranch houses contain exhibits dedicated to early ranching history in these

parts and others to much earlier human habitation going back several thousand years.

Sarcee Peoples Museum

The Sarcee Peoples Museum is found on the Sarcee Indian Reservation (on the southwest edge of Calgary at the western end of Anderson Road). The Sarcee people have a mysterious heritage. They are actually Beaver Indians but a group broke away and moved south to this country centuries ago. Despite a complete language difference with the local Blackfoot federation tribes, the Sarcee people lived here in peace.

Sailing on Glenmore Reservoir

Olympic Plaza: centre of activity in winter and summer

Spruce Meadows

Just south of Calgary, off Highway 22 west of Highway 6, Spruce Meadows stands out from the fields as a piece of the old world parachuted into the new. It is an equestrian and show-jumping facility of world rank and the world's best dressage and show jumping horses and riders come here to compete for the laurels of their sport. Like so many Calgary attractions, Spruce Meadows owes its existence to the public spiritedness and dedication of one family: the Southern (known to the world also as the force behind the multinational firm, Atco).

Spruce Meadows hosts national and international tournaments as well as tournaments for younger riders and horses.

The Olympic Facilities

Where the Trans-Canada Highway leaves Calgary to the west, you will find Canada Olympic Park. The ski-jumping, luge, bobsled and some specialty downhill events of the XVth Winter Olympics were held at this site. Here you will also find the Olympic Hall of Fame, an exhibition of photographs, artifacts, videos and other displays paying homage to winter olympians, past and present.

If you continue on to the mountains you can complete your tour of 1988 winter olympic facilities at two locations: Nakiska and the Canmore Nordic Centre. Nakiska is in the Kananaskis Valley 55 driving minutes from Calgary. It is the mountain on which the downhill and slalom skiing competitions were held. The Canmore Nordic Centre is on the

The Calgary Stampede, the greatest outdoor show on earth. Cowboys and visitors come from all over America for ten days of carnival atmosphere. Chuckwagon races, a world class rodeo, the Indian Village, street dances, parades and pancake breakfasts all add up to hospitality and fun for all ages.

Olympic Hall of Fame

mountain above the town of Canmore, 60 driving minutes west of Calgary on the Trans-Canada. This was the cross-country skiing and nordic combined venue at the '88 Winter Olympics.

Cities become great through a combination of their prosperity and the commitment of their citizens. Calgary has both. The richest Calgary millionaire and the average joe who donates volunteer time to the Stampede have in common their willingness to give in order that Calgary will look good to the world, in order that

certain Calgary traditions are upheld and maintained. For a city of its size Calgary is rich in lore. Everything that it has ever been — wilderness, frontier town, ranching centre, oil boomtown and, most recently, Olympic city — it has held onto tightly through the media of parks, festivals and museums. Calgary is a city of strong identity, as well-known as any city of its size on the North American continent.

Calaway Park, ten minutes west of Calgary, is Canada's first major Theme Park. Live shows, attractions, food and beverage facilities and fifteen major rides attract all members of the family.

Canada Olympic Park with its Olympic Hall of Fame, ski jump tower, luge track and bob sleigh run is part of the legacy of the Winter Olympics. The other part of that legacy is the volunteer spirit of Calgarians which made the Olympic experience happen.

The Dinosaur Tour

*T*he prairie stretches out before you, the distant corners of wheat fields seeming to touch the sky. The horizon is an infinite view to the east, west, north and south. It surrounds you, envelops you.

On this expanse of prairie any roll in the terrain is a welcome change and when the land begins to undulate, it grips your attention. Suddenly the prairies fall away, revealing a gaping valley of unusual hills and mounds: the badlands of the Red Deer River Valley. The hills loom up beside the highway. Some are cone-shaped and steep. Many are tiered, with layers of rock and soil in greys, browns, and tinges of orange. Some are rounded, their ruddy, cracked and furrowed surfaces like the hides of the great beasts whose remains they conceal.

This tour takes you through prairie and badlands, to frontier coal mining towns and internationally-known sites for dinosaur fossil discoveries. The first leg of the Red Deer River Valley tour begins at Dinosaur Provincial Park, moves through Bassano, and on to Drumheller. The second leg takes in points east and west of Drumheller, including the Tyrrell Museum of Palaeontology, former coal mining towns, sites of historical and recreational significance, and some of the most interesting terrain in Canada.

Dinosaur Provincial Park

Wind whines through the stubble of brush over a dry badlands valley, its whispers joined only by the incessant creaking of crickets and the occasional clacking of grasshoppers' wings. Below you the hills are naked to the dry wind and hot sun, their surfaces cracked and nearly barren. But there's something intriguing about this forlorn landscape, some unseen attraction.

The sedimentary rock at the park is 100 times softer than the Rockies. The Valley of Castles is an excellent example of nature's powers of erosion.

There, beneath the surface of the earth, rising slowly and silently from their shallow graves, are secrets of the earth's prehistoric past: the fossils. Scientists have identified fossils in the park from 35 different species of dinosaurs, making it one of the richest caches of dinosaur bones in the world. In 1979, UNESCO declared Dinosaur Provincial Park a World Heritage Site.

The Tyrrell Museum has established a field station at the park as a base for palaeontologists working in the area. The station also houses interpretive facilities for visitors, including displays, theatre presentations and a number of programs for adults and children. Visitors can hike or tour by bus through parts of the park's badlands which are not restricted-access areas.

This area is a natural habitat to many animals and bird species and in fact acts as a refuge, an oasis in the surrounding dry prairie. The Red Deer River Valley, provider of moisture and plant life, is a breeding and feeding ground for such animals as white-tail or mule-tail deer, beavers, coyotes, cottontail and jackrabbits and a host of others. The Cottonwood Trail at Dinosaur Park offers excellent birdwatching opportunities as there are over 130 species in the area. Watch particularly for bluebirds, meadowlarks, orioles and avocets.

Take your time exploring: there are overnight camping facilities just below the field office on the Red Deer River. Near the campground you'll see the homesteading cabin of John Ware, Alberta's legendary black cowboy.

If you identify a significant fossil location, you may receive an official Fossil Finder Certificate.

Remember that fossils you may find are part of Alberta's natural heritage and are protected by law. Please examine them, but leave them for others to study and enjoy. Major discoveries should be reported to the Tyrrell Museum at 823-7707.

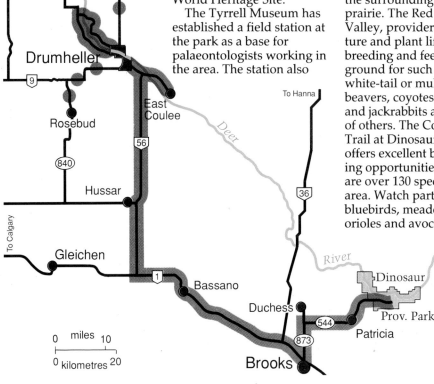

A History of the Land

Geology can open doors to billions of years of history: some rocks tell of prehistoric inland seas while others recall coastal beaches, or bear the scars of glaciation. Rocks reveal the land's personality, power and ancient past and, like the rings of a tree, tell much about the environments of different eras.

The whole environment of 70 million years ago would appear alien today. Imagine yourself at the edge of a vast inland sea fed by a wide, sluggish river and fringed by sandy shorelines, swamps and washed-out lowlands. The air is warm and moist: seasons do not exist as we know them today. The shape of the continent is much different, and the area is farther south in latitude.

There are no Rocky Mountains to the west, but volcanos often rumble from the distant southwest, occasionally spilling lava and ash into the area. In the water, an array of strange life competes for food and survival, while at the water's edge, crocodiles and a host of other reptiles move amid a tangle of growth. On land there are moss-draped forests and here, and in open spaces, the dinosaurs prevail.

Toward the end of the dinosaur's reign, the earth's crust buckled where the Rocky Mountains now stand. The mountains were pushed up slowly but the pressure caused rock to crack and crumble. Silt, pulverized rock and mud washed into rivers and streams which carried much of these materials into what is now the Drumheller

Plant Life

Certain plants have evolved specifically for life in the badlands. The semi-arid climate, dry, sandy soils and the constant forces of erosion discourage most growth which is otherwise common on prairies. Trees require a great deal of water and are generally found only near lakes

and rivers. Some plants, like the prickly pear cactus and dryland grasses, however, thrive in badlands environments. Storing moisture in broad, flat stems, the cactus endures the long dry spells which are common in the valley.

area. This erosion is still visible in the layers of crumbly sandstone and mudstone in the badlands.

Millions of years later, changes in climate triggered a series of cold spells throughout the world. Ice accumulated on the land and most animals from this area migrated or disappeared. When the climate warmed again, the ice sheet broke up and huge glacial blocks moved over the land, gouging deep valleys and bulldozing rock and soils.

The badlands of the Red Deer River Valley are the product of recent glacial action and meltwater runoff, along with numerous other factors. The semi-arid climate in the Red Deer River Valley does much to maintain the badlands. Minimal rainfall in the area discourages plant growth, and the lack of vegetation allows erosion which is an important factor in badlands formation. In all its forms, water is the most powerful

erosional element, etching deep furrows in the hills, forever sculpting and re-sculpting the faces of the valley.

Bentonite Soils

Badlands landforms owe their unusual looks to bentonite, a rock ash from ancient volcanos which erupted to the southwest. The ash fallout washed into rivers and streams, accumulating layer upon layer, sometimes bonding with sand or mud. Bentonite makes an unstable bonding agent, as you can see from the crumbly sandstone and mudstone in today's badlands. Its unstable nature accounts for the incredible rate of erosion here. With each rainfall, the surfaces of hills are washed away, at the rate of up to 1 centimetre per year. This whitish, powdery clay is very slippery when wet and at one time was used by pioneers as soap.

Drumheller and area were once covered with water from the retreating glaciers; about 20,000 years ago.

The field tools of the palaeontology trade have remained virtually unchanged since the early 1900s. Patience, perseverance and a good deal of perspiration are still needed to free the fossil from the rock.

Buried Treasures

Dinosaur bones, coal mining, oil and natural gas all originated in prehistoric times through fossilization. Long before the advent of human beings, the area was at the edge of a large inland sea, abundant with plant growth. Rotting vegetation accumulated layer upon layer and was buried in mud, sand and plant matter. Sealed off from the air, and with the combined effects of compression, heat and time, this accumulation was converted to coal.

Coal was first discovered here by explorer Peter Fidler, almost a century ago. But it wasn't until the construction of a major rail line through the area that transporting the coal became possible. More than 124 coal mines have operated in the Red Deer River Valley since the first mine opened in 1912. Coal mining was dirty and dangerous work; the pay was not exceptional. The large mines operated day and night to meet the demand for coal and Red Deer River Valley coal was shipped across the country to heat homes and fuel locomotives. The last coal mine in the valley stopped production in 1977.

Although crude oil and natural gas have similar origins to coal, they were formed much earlier when the sea extended over much of what is now Alberta. Remains of sea life buried and compacted in coral reefs are believed to be responsible for Alberta's extensive oil and gas fields.

Hanna Pioneer Museum

Since it opened in 1964, the Hanna Museum has built a reputation as one of the finest pioneer museums in Alberta. The main building contains a wealth of artifacts, and the expanded Pioneer Village includes a one-room rural school, a railway station complete with railway and caboose, a pioneer home and store, set in authentic surroundings. Hanna is about one hour north of Dinosaur Provincial Park on Highway 36 or 40 minutes northeast of Drumheller on Highway 9.

Historic building in Pioneer Village

Prairie Oasis Park

Just south of Hanna on Highway 36, Prairie Oasis Park has been developed next to the Sherness Power Plant. Waterskiing, canoeing, and picnic tables are available, and visitors can tour the power plant.

Water-skiing at Prairie Oasis Park

The Bassano Dam and Crawling Valley Reservoir are part of the Eastern Irrigation District which stretches past Brooks. As a result of the irrigation system, the dam and reservoir have been turned into a recreational area now stocked with rainbow trout. Boating, sailing and camping facilities are also available.

Exploring Dinosaur Provincial Park

HOODOO TRAIL

Wayne

There were six mines along this road at one time, and the narrow valley was crowded with homes and businesses. The road, which crosses the river 11 times in six kilometres, was built to reach the coal mine and the thriving town of Wayne: which, in the 1920s and 30s, boasted a population of more than 2,000.

The original Last Chance Saloon in the Rosedeer Hotel, built in 1913, is one of the few remaining landmarks to remind Wayne's 70 residents of the boom years. The hotel and saloon have changed little over the years and are still open for business.

Rosedale

In 1914 when Star Mine in Rosedale opened, men and coal were regularly transported across the Red Deer River by slings on a cable system. These slings were used for almost 20 years, until 1931 when a swinging bridge was built. Star Mine

has since been buried in a rock slide, but you can still cross the bridge and see the remains of the mine.

Hoodoos

Welcome to the moon. This garden of strangely sculptured towers of rock will remind you of old science fiction movies as you walk the trail north of the road. Native people described the hoodoos as petrified giants who came alive at night and hurled rocks down at intruders. As you can see by the exposed sides of hills, the rock and soil occur in layers. Some layers are more resistant than others to erosion and the caps on

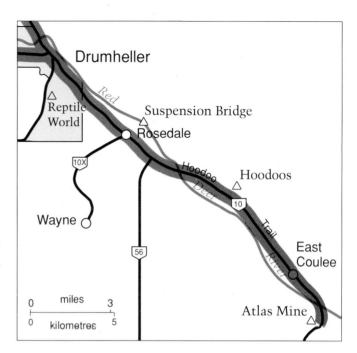

Notice the caprock of hard sandstone on top of the Hoodoo. Hoodoos range from the size of your thumb to many metres high.

top of the hoodoo formations are of relatively hard rock. They act as umbrellas, sheltering the pillars of softer sandstone beneath from rain and sun. Without their caps, the pillars would have washed away long ago.

East Coulee

In the 1920s and 30s the town was crowded with small homes built by miners. Dirt roads were busy with cars and trucks. In 1930, the burgeoning

community built the school now housing the East Coulee Museum. Creaking wood floors, and the classroom with its chalkboards and old wooden desks, still stir the memories. The museum also houses a tearoom and craft store, photo exhibits and a small mining display.

Atlas Mine

Most of the mines that once drew thousands of people to this area are now buried in rock slides, or have been closed, with only the echoes of falling rock sounding in their dark and empty caverns. The Atlas Mine, however, is one of the last of its kind in North America with its tipple rising to meet the surrounding landscape. The Atlas Mine is in the process of restoration and has opened some of its original buildings for visitors. Soon the echoes of footsteps will once again sound in the mine as the Atlas staff prepares to conduct tours into the shaft. One of the last large mines in the valley, the slag heaps of impure coal still smoulder on the site; some have

Notice the different coal layers in the cliffs as you cross the Suspension Bridge.

The city of Drumheller is at the heart of the Dinosaur Tour and marks the starting point of the Dinosaur Trail beginning on the next page.

Drumheller's name was decided in a 1911 flip of the coin between Sam Drumheller, a Washington entrepreneur, and a homesteader named Thomas Greentree. If things had turned out differently, you might now be in Greentree's Crossing instead of in Drumheller.

Dinosaur and Fossil Museum

Located in downtown Drumheller, the Dinosaur and Fossil Museum features the L.A. Duncan Collection, one man's lifetime work. Fossil, marine life and Indian artifacts, found in the hills of the Red Deer River Valley, are displayed, along with a 10 metre Edmontosaurus skeleton.

Reptile World

Live crocodiles, lizards, cobras, frogs, turtles and even a giant iguana are some of the 250 animals living at Reptile World, Canada's largest public living reptile display. Reptile World is located next to the tour information booth on Highway 9 south. Special tours are available for schools and other interested groups.

Prehistoric Parks

This compound is a fascinating exhibit of life-sized dinosaur reproductions. Children love to roam in typical badlands scenery where the dinosaurs seem to come to life. The park is located on the South Dinosaur Trail.

Prehistoric Park is set in a typical Badlands setting. Life-sized dinosaur models are scattered throughout the fifty-six hectare park.

been smoking since the mine first opened in 1911. Do not approach the heaps if you see or smell smoke, as the black crust may have burned-out caverns, or hot coals, beneath. Atlas Mine is accessible from the gravel road turnoff on the north side of the highway, just as you enter East Coulee.

Drumheller

The town of Drumheller, with its 7,000 people, is small enough for ease of exploration, yet large enough to provide amenities and entertainment for visitors. There are comfortable motels as well as campsites, and a small sandy riverside beach at Newcastle Recreation Area. A museum displays Indian artifacts and fossils, providing a quick primer on dinosaurs and the area's history and geology, and life-sized models of dinosaurs grace Prehistoric Park.

Atlas Mine, one of the last tipples in North America

Centrosaurus (Sharp Point Reptile)

DINOSAUR TRAIL

The Tyrrell Museum of Palaeontology attracts over five hundred thousand visitors each year.

Homestead Antique Museum

This privately-owned antique exhibit, which has an admission charge, is known for its diversity. The collection runs from old musical instruments, Indian artifacts, and antique lighters to farm implements, trucks, cars and even a stuffed, two-headed calf.

Midland Provincial Park

The site of the Midland #1 and #2 Mines, one of the first in the valley, today features interpretive walks, a chance to tour the old mine office, and a wooded riverside pathway at McMullen Island. The mine closed in 1940 but old mining tools are still in evidence.

Tyrrell Museum

A good museum prompts as many questions as it answers. The Tyrrell Museum of Palaeontology provides clear and fascinating information on our 4.6 billion-year-old planet. It is a fossil museum but, in helping us to understand and appreciate fossils, it also encourages us to consider the tremendous expanse of time before human civilization began and our own staggering insignificance. Some of the world's best fossils are displayed in this fascinating setting. Exhibits and

Approximately 90% of the fossilized bones found in the Red Deer Badlands are about 75 million years old. Most are related to the duck-billed dinosaur species.

computer simulations intrigue children and adults as they participate in demonstrations of the fossilization process. The museum gives visitors a taste of the excitement and fascination Joseph Tyrrell (Teer ell) must have felt in 1884 when, nearby, he found the bones of the carnivorous Albertosaurus.

All plants in the Tyrrell Museum's palaeoconservancy are relatives of actual plants that grew here when the area was an inland sea. They have been gathered from all corners of the world to be included in the attractive exhibit.

(Map)

To Hanna, Trochu

Bleriot Ferry

9

North

Red

Dinosaur

Horsethief Canyon Viewpoint

South

Viewpoint

575

Dinosaur

River

Trail

Tyrrell Museum

Trail

Tourist Information

Nacmine

Homestead Antique Museum

Prehistoric Park

Tourist Information

Reptile World

River

9

Drumheller

To Calgary

Horseshoe Canyon

miles

0   5

0   10
kilometres

The Bleriot Ferry has been serving travellers for decades.

Rosebud Dinner Theatre

On Secondary Road 840 just south of Highway 9, the small town of Rosebud presents a most unique dinner theatre throughout the spring and summer. Focusing on the history of the West, productions take place in a pioneer church which has been converted to a theatre. Reservations are recommended.

Rosebud Museum and Dinner Theatre

Horsethief Canyon

Folds and bends in this canyon provided an ideal place for thieves in the early 1900s to hide their stolen horses. From the top of the canyon, one can view areas that contain ancient fossilized oyster beds, and take in a spectacular view of the badlands valley, sculpted by water and erosion.

Bleriot Ferry

Built in 1913, the Bleriot Ferry is now one of the oldest operating cable ferries of its kind in Alberta. Pulled by cables and pulleys, it takes a small number of vehicles across the river at regular intervals. On the south side of the river and just upstream from Munson Campground, a major fossil discovery was made in 1923 when the fossilized bones of a duck-billed dinosaur called Edmontosaurus were unearthed.

Lookout Point

From the west, you'll have a sweeping view of the winding Red Deer River and the green valley floor. Be cautious near the roadsides, as they can be slippery when wet. Just upstream from this point Indians once herded buffalo over cliffs, and teepee rings in the area indicate that Native people favoured this location as sites for hunting camps. As you head east along South Dinosaur Trail, you'll pass Nacmine and Newcastle, once rough and tumble mining towns with reputations for bootlegging and gambling exploits.

Tyrannosaurus (Tyrant Lizard)

Horseshoe Canyon

Make time for this fifteen minute drive off South Dinosaur Trail and south on #9. Walk the well-worn trails into the badlands formations of spectacular Horseshoe Canyon, and complete your tour of the Red Deer River Valley.

Often described as a miniature Grand Canyon, a short hike in the canyon will open a strange new world to the visitor.

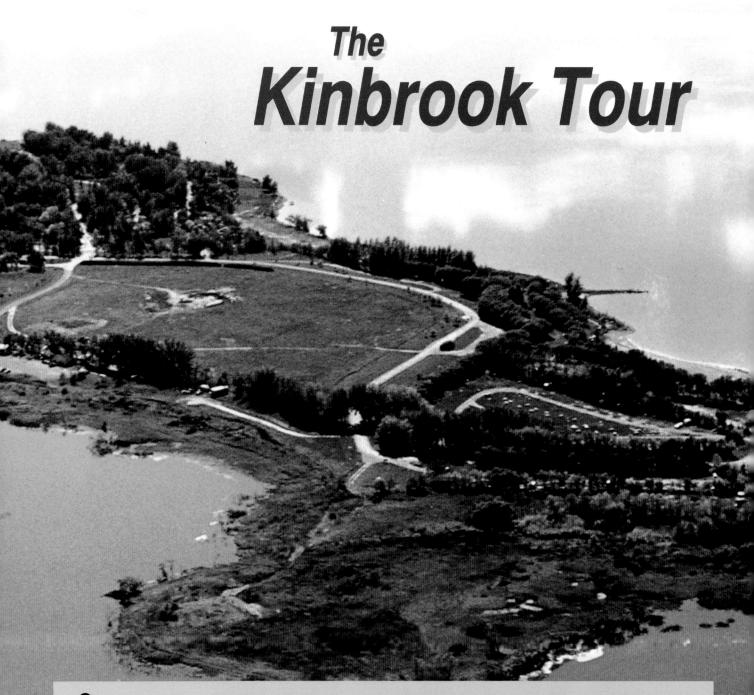

The Kinbrook Tour

On either side of the road, as far as the eye can see, vast seas of alfafa, barley and wheat are smoothed in waves by the unencumbered wind. A jackrabbit dashes into a shrub, startling a pheasant hiding there. Ahead, a farmer on a slow-moving tractor waves you by with a smile.

On this semi-arid land, rainfall during the growing season averages only 150 mm, and drying winds and blazing sun compound the need for moisture. By constructing an aqueduct, man-made lakes and irrigation ditches, farmers have managed to conserve enough water to maintain a viable agricultural industry.

The Kinbrook tour tells the story of hardy homesteaders who first looked upon the prairie and saw not a dry expanse of wild grass, but possibility. They ignored the hasty conclusion of British explorer Captain John Palliser who, in 1862, reported the area a wasteland. He was proven wrong. This area now supports a plenitude of crops, a large beef industry, and one of the largest feed operations in Canada. As well, visitors can enjoy a vacation in the oasis, both in the town of Brooks and at grassy Kinbrook Island Provincial Park, where visitors swim, water ski, fish and windsurf.

Irrigation

One of the driest areas of Alberta boasts a thriving agricultural industry, producing vegetables, greenhouse crops, fruits, grains, honey and livestock. Irrigation is the key. The 5,990 square kilometres surrounding Brooks form one of North America's largest irrigation districts.

In the early 1900s, the CPR began a costly irrigation program in the Brooks area which included construction of a dam at Bassano, an extensive canal system and an aqueduct near Brooks. The plan worked. Settlers moved in quickly, but because of the high cost of irrigation projects, the CPR could not fulfil its long-term plans for the "Eastern Block." The project was handed over to farmers in 1935 and renamed the Eastern Irrigation District.

Today, the Eastern Irrigation District meets many needs: requirements for domestic water and those of wildlife habitats, recreation and tourism, are all supported by the economic generator of water. Water has provided a favourable environment for a wide variety of birds and mammals such as the Canada goose, the mallard duck, and the fleet pronghorn antelope. Water creates opportunities for swimming, boating, fishing and picnicking at Lake Newell, and it nourishes the soil to produce crops that yield four to five times the wheat and feed produced in non-irrigated areas. Bordered on the north by the Red Deer River, and on the south by the Bow River, the irrigation district creates an oasis in the surrounding prairie dryland, and brings economic stability to the area.

Since 1935, the irrigation system has been financially supported solely by its users, receiving government assistance only for the rehabilitation program. Today, the area includes twelve water reservoirs, the

Irrigation has created an oasis in the prairie for the town of Brooks and surrounding area.

Bassano Dam, 1,900 kilometres of canals, 1,500 kilometres of surface drains and 2,497 water control structures. Individual farmers use mobile sprinkler systems, dikes, ditches and furrows to distribute the water. There are presently more than 98,800 hectares of irrigated land in the system.

On the Trans-Canada

Brooks Wildlife Centre

Adjacent to Tillebrook Park, ten kilometres east of Brooks, visitors can tour the areas of the wildlife centre where ring-necked pheasants are hatched and raised, then released throughout southern Alberta for recreational hunting and viewing. Over 100,000 pheasant chicks are produced each year. Many of the chicks are passed on to 4-H and Fish and Game Clubs who enjoy raising the pheasants and then releasing them when they reach 16 weeks.

The centre also receives more than 100 injured and orphaned birds of prey each year and works to heal and then restore them to their natural environments.

Indoor and outdoor interpretive facilities at the centre include audio-visual

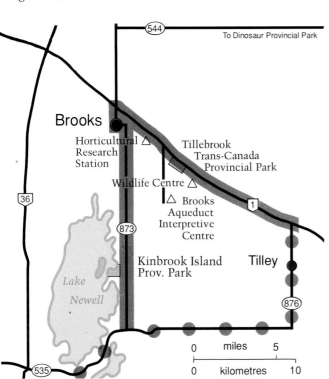

The ring-necked pheasant, which originally came from China, was released in the Brooks area 1908-1909. This game bird thrives on wheat and barley, and is well protected in the thick cover of trees and shrubs along the irrigation canals.

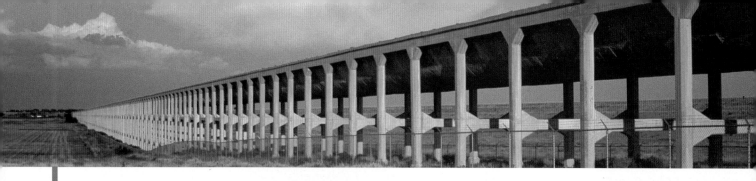

presentations, mounted specimens of wildlife, and an egg collection. Game birds and waterfowl can be seen in outdoor pens and guided tours are available.

Tillebrook Provincial Park

About 120 clean, treed campsites at Tillebrook provide the finest in civilized camping. Paved roads, neatly manicured lawns, laundry facilities, showers, and a picnic shelter with a gas stove make for luxury camping.

Aqueduct

To encourage settlement in the Brooks area, the CPR, between 1909 and 1914, constructed dams, 48,000 kilometres of ditches, and a suspended canal modelled after the great aqueducts of Rome.

Stretching 3.2 kilometres, the Brooks aqueduct was the CPR's major project. It was designed and built to overcome a major problem: how to deliver water over a 3-kilometre wide, 18-metre deep coulee, in order to serve the communities of

Exploring the Horticultural Research Centre

Tilley, Patricia, One Tree, and Millicent.

The concrete trough, 4.6 metres wide, once carried 19.5 cubic metres of water per second, from Lake Newell to high fields southeast of Brooks. Completed in 1914, and averaging three stories in height, it stands on hundreds of pillars: a testimony to the feats of irrigation farming and the engineering miracles of its day. Although no longer in use, this forerunner of the country's largest irrigation system has been declared a national historic site.

Guided tours and information on the aqueduct and the area are available throughout the summer.

Horticultural Research Centre

About five kilometres southeast of Brooks just off the Trans-Canada Highway, trees exotic to Alberta sway in the breeze. The air is perfumed with cedar, juniper and colourful flowers. Trails wind

The Centre tests over 30 different varieties of wheat.

through gardens landscaped with shrubs, hedges, rocks, ferns and roses.

In 1,260 square metres of greenhouse space, research, designed to help commercial greenhouse growers in Alberta, is carried on. Studies are also being conducted on non-traditional crops to encourage diversification of the province's agricultural products. Tours are conducted summer weekdays at scheduled times, and a cook shelter and picnic area are on site. A unique Field Day in August attracts 3,000 people.

Tillebrook Campground

Forty minutes from Brooks

North of the Trans-Canada

Petting Zoo and Patricia Hotel

Just a few kilometres northeast of Brooks (Highway 544) on the way to Dinosaur Park, take the opportunity to touch llamas, pigmy goats, exotic pheasants, miniature horses, canaries, finches, budgies and a host of other animals and birds. The Whispering Creek Petting Ranch is open from early June to the end of September.

At Patricia, a few kilometres further down the road, the Patricia Hotel provides the western flavour of an historic era. Many of the "brands" on the walls date back 75 years and reflect the area's long tradition of ranching and agriculture. The Patricia Hotel, built in the 1920s, is noted for its buffalo burgers and buffalo steaks.

Dinosaur Provincial Park

Dinosaur Provincial Park, a world heritage site 48 km north of Brooks, is one of the most unusual dinosaur settings in North America. The park offers tours and a first-class interpretive station. Please refer to the Dinosaur Tour for detailed information.

South of the Trans-Canada

Brooks

Before the Canadian Pacific Railroad, before the North-West Mounted Police and before the Blood and Blackfoot Indians hunted buffalo across the prairie, dinosaurs roamed freely throughout the area.

Warm shallow water at Lake Newell

A four ton replica of one of those giant beasts guards the entrance to the Brooks and District Museum. Here, the more recent history of the area is lovingly preserved. In buildings of historic interest and in more modern surroundings, the museum displays artifacts from Brooks' colourful past.

Today, Brooks' population of about 10,000 is supported primarily by

Lake Newell is Canada's largest man-made lake.

retail business, water, livestock, oil and agricultural activity. It is also home to one of North America's largest summer rodeos. Surrounded by 0.6 million hectares of farms and ranch land, its residents know the value of water. Brooks is an oasis of cottonwood and poplar trees, and its tractor pulls, farmers' markets, fall fairs and hospitality make it an authentic country town.

Windsurfing and sailing - powered by prairie winds

Kinbrook Island Provincial Park/ Lake Newell

Lake Newell, Canada's largest man-made lake, functions primarily as a water reservoir for the Eastern Irrigation District. Besides providing water for

Testing one's own stamina

farmland, Lake Newell beckons visitors with a variety of water activities including sunbathing, swimming, windsurfing, water skiing and fishing. The treed park has more than 200 shaded campsites and a lot of picnic tables.

A variety of wild birds, including pelicans and cormorants, are also attracted to the area.

Adjacent to the park are two new bird sanctuaries, Swen Bayer Peninsula and Kinbrook Marsh. The Wetlands Trail provides visitors first-hand experience with wildfowl habitats.

Wildlife Habitat

Most ducks in Alberta nest on dry uplands which surround wetlands, such as those at the edge of a slough. However, due to drought, the edges of sloughs are being tilled to crop, resulting in the loss of these habitats. The 1970s and 1980s have seen the reduction of duck nests to ten

percent of their former levels. Organizations such as Ducks Unlimited work with farmers, municipalities, irrigation districts and governments to build choice wetland sites such as those you see in the area of Brooks. Without the development of high quality fowl habitats, ducks, geese, swans, pelicans and a host of other waterfowl, and their predators, would be doomed to extinction.

A Vacation Oasis

Nestled within the broad expanse of dryland prairie, the Kinbrook Tour offers diversity in an oasis. Water, wildlife, recreation, agriculture and dinosaurs combine to generate experiences that will keep you coming back, time after time.

The park and area provides much-needed natural habitat.

The
Buffalo Trail

*T*o travel Alberta's Buffalo Trail is to follow in the distant wake of the great buffalo herds that first wore this north-south path. Along this route, Highway 41, the accent is on landscape and one discovery you will make is that the prairie is not one but several landscapes.

South of Medicine Hat the Buffalo Trail climbs into the Cypress Hills, one of the most extraordinary landscape features on the entire continent. In the cool, high Cypress Hills much of the vegetation is shared not with the surrounding plains but with the far off mountains.

North of Medicine Hat, the form is prairie grassland, home to the gopher and the pronghorn antelope. Such undisturbed prairie is a rarity in today's extensively cultivated West.

The third distinct landscape visitors will see along the Buffalo Trail is found right in the city of Medicine Hat, and that is river valley. Medicine Hat has long appreciated the beauty and uniqueness of this riverside habitat and has celebrated it with a series of urban parks: rural landscapes within a bustling city.

Medicine Hat

Medicine Hat is a city of surprises and the first surprise is the suddenness with which the traveller comes upon it. From all directions, stretches of lonesome prairie precede the city. Suddenly, the South Saskatchewan River valley yawns open before you and Medicine Hat appears, the thriving hub of a broad trading region stretching east into Saskatchewan and south to the U.S. border.

The next surprise is how different the city is from the country around it. At the heart of the prairie, Medicine Hat is anything but flat. Its streets ascend and traverse steep valley walls and coulee banks. Viewpoints abound and the vistas are striking: here a twin-spired church, there a peninsula of natural cottonwoods; sheer cliffs, broad railyards, narrow gully systems. Medicine Hat has made the most of its beautiful valley and coulees through a series of parks, each with its own character.

Visitors may also be surprised at how old and established Medicine Hat is, and how much of the early city is incorporated in its modern face. The arrival of the Canadian Pacific Railway and a wise decision by the town to invest in the local gas reservoirs led to swift urban development at Medicine Hat just after the turn of the century. To this day, the railway and city-owned natural gas give Medicine Hat an edge in attracting and maintaining industry.

Medicine Hat is the hub of a broad interprovincial trading region.

The History of a City

Medicine Hat has played a key role in the history of southern Alberta. A walk around downtown illustrates that history and the pride local residents take in it.

Eighteen hundred and eighty-three was a pivotal year in the history of Medicine Hat. The steam engines that powered 19th century trains had a great thirst for water and on the dry prairies that thirst was hard to quench. In 1883, at a siding called Langevin near Medicine Hat, the CPR water-well diggers drilled for water and came up with natural gas. This was the first discovery of natural gas in Alberta.

Visitors to Medicine Hat may not be able to see the underground sources of the natural gas but they certainly can see signs of the turn-of-the-century prosperity natural gas brought to the city. A "Historic Walking Tour" guidebook is available at the tourist information centre to help you find key points of interest. One of the highlights of that tour is St. Patrick's Roman Catholic Church at the north end of Findlay Bridge. With its 51 metre high, twin Gothic towers, this church is the dominant feature of many Medicine Hat views. Built in 1913, the church is a fine example of Gothic Revival architecture.

At the opposite end of Findlay Bridge, you will find the Medicine Hat City Hall. This beautiful,

Medicine Hat City Hall - the design that received the Governor General's Medal for Architecture.

modern building cannot be called historic but it is certainly history in the making; its dramatic design has already been recognized by a national award, the Governor General's Medal for Architecture.

West of City Hall is the stately 1919 Provincial Court House. Enter through the elaborate stone-carved entrance for a look at the marble foyer and the winding staircase with its brass and oak bannister.

Recreating the past

Across First Street from the Court House you will see a fine Victorian home known as the Ewart-Duggan House. Built in 1887 for John Ewart, a local businessman, it is one of the oldest brick residences still standing in Alberta.

Elsewhere in downtown, you will find three of the city's oldest churches: Saint John's Presbyterian (1902), Fifth Avenue United Church (1912) and Saint Barnabas Anglican Church (also 1912).

The railway tracks are the eastern boundary of downtown and the old Canadian Pacific Railway (CPR) Station is another of the city's historic sites. It was built in two stages, in 1906 and 1911, and represents a style the CPR

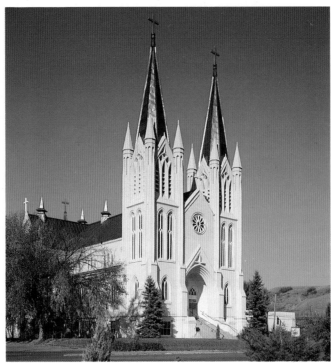

St Patrick's church overlooks the city.

developed for its western Canadian stations in the period. In the 19th Century, at approximately this spot, a black bear named Nancy was kept penned alongside the tracks as a spectacle for travellers.

Medicine Hat Museum and Art Gallery

Close by the intersection of Highway 3 and the Trans-Canada Highway, you will

Learning to weave at the Medicine Hat Museum and Art Gallery.

find the Medicine Hat Museum and Art Gallery. Through permanent exhibits, the museum tells the story of Medicine Hat's growth and development: Native history, the open range ranching era and the homestead era. The art gallery is a national exhibition centre featuring travelling exhibitions from across Canada. The institution provides a variety of educational programs for adults and children which bring alive the city's cultural history: everything from heritage festivals to Victorian Christmases.

Medalta Potteries

The Medalta Potteries historic site is found in the area just south of Strathcona Island Park. You will know you are in the right part of town by the street names: Porcelain, Clay, Wood, Steel, Medalta and Industrial. The place to begin a walking tour is the site's interpretive centre within the National Porcelain warehouse.

The stoneware pottery industry became viable at Medicine Hat in 1915 when Medalta Stoneware Limited found a source of suitable clay in Saskatchewan. This venture was a major success. Medalta's slogan in the 1920s was "Canadian-made Stoneware from Canadian Clay, made by Canadian Workmen and financed by Canadian Capital." The quality of the goods plus this nationalist appeal brought about almost total replacement of American crockery by Medalta stoneware in homes and businesses across Canada.

Medalta's meteoric rise was stalled in 1929 by the double whammy of the Depression and a switch to glass in jugs and soft drink bottles. Medalta responded with a new line of lamp bases, vases, plaques and ash trays. During World

Street lights powered by natural gas.

War II, the company supplied dinnerware to the Canadian Forces. A series of setbacks after the war led to the company's closure in 1954.

Medalta pottery is one of the most sought-after collectibles in the world and, here at Medicine Hat, you can see the manufacturing buildings and beehive kilns where it was made.

Parks and Play

Many have used the word "oasis" to describe Medicine Hat and one of the city's surprising characteristics certainly is how much greenspace it contains and how that green contrasts with the golden prairie beyond the city limits. A theme for Medicine Hat's extensive park system could be "a park for every purpose" or "a different purpose for every park."

Cottonwood tree shaped by the wind and terrain.

Police Point Park

The focus at Police Point, a large peninsular park on the river, is on nature in its undisturbed riverbottom glory. This carefully preserved cottonwood forest is truly an inner city wilderness, home to deer and many other wildlife species. The name harkens back to the Mounted Police outpost built at this location in 1883. Police Point's interpretive centre has exhibits, a resource library, a film theatre and a staff of park interpreters all dedicated to a fuller understanding of this river valley habitat: an ecology very different from that found on the prairie upland. Eight kilometres of shaded pathway wind among the twisted cottonwoods and, whether you bike it, hike it or ski it, you are likely to forget that you are in a city at all.

Notice the differences in vegetation between the prairie landscape and the coulees in the city.

Strathcona Island Park

Directly across the river from Police Point is Strathcona Island Park where nature has a more manicured appearance and where the focus is on outdoor recreation in all seasons. In addition to its greens and pathways, Strathcona Island has a lake which can be enjoyed from canoes and paddleboats available at the park's Heritage Pavilion. A lakeside deck is outfitted with umbrella-shaded picnic tables. There is also a large playground with a water play centre. In the winter months, the frozen lake is taken over by skaters, the pathways by winter joggers and cross-country skiers.

Although the railway siding downtown is the official birthplace of the city, the stretch of river between Police Point and Strathcona Island deserves credit as the birthplace of the city's name. Whether a powerful Blackfoot medicine man lost his head-dress in the river or whether a starving Cree man sacrificed his wife to the river to get a powerful medicine bonnet, the legendary happening is said to have taken place where the river bends between the two parks.

Echo Dale Park

The key word to describe Echo Dale Park is water. To get there, follow Highway 3

Hands-on exhibit at Echo Dale farm

west and turn right on Holsom Road just beyond the edge of the city. This leads you back to the South Saskatchewan and to a garden of water delights. Echo Dale has a clean well-supervised beach with concessions and change rooms. It has a fishing lake stocked with trout. Paddleboats and canoes are available. There are also

Echo Dale Park - a man-made lake in a natural setting.

picnic sites aplenty and a coulee system to explore. In addition, the Echo Dale Farm with the historic Wolfery House and the Ajax Coal Mine are two more chances to look back on the turn-of-the-century history of this area.

Strathcona Park focuses on outdoor year-round recreation.

Summer theatre at Kin Coulee

Kin Coulee Park

Kin Coulee Park is found in the coulee of Seven Persons Creek beside the Trans-Canada Highway. In the ravine systems and coulee flats, the emphasis is on family fun: picnics, baseball, football and frisbee. There is an exciting track for the BMX enthusiast. In winter, the park is a favourite haunt of cross-country skiers and tobogganers who can gather in the warming hut between runs.

Kin Coulee also has a great historical significance. There is an ancient graveyard and the Seven Persons Coulee has been declared a provincial historic site for the archaeological finds that have been made there. Seven Persons Creek had great significance to famous frontiersman Kootenai Brown. When Brown first crossed the Canadian prairies in 1865, he and his fellow travellers were ambushed in their camp on Seven Persons Creek and Brown took an arrow in the back. He washed his wound with a cup of turpentine and, after healing, continued on to Fort Garry.

Gas City Campground

For the campers in the crowd, the Gas City Campground, found just off the Trans-Canada Highway above the South Saskatchewan, is an ideal facility. It is handy to the highway and minutes away from all the city's attractions. Whatever your style of camping, tent, RV or trailer, you will find full facilities at Gas City.

City of Water and Parks

Though the major parks of Medicine Hat are mentioned above, there are over 70 smaller parks scattered throughout the city. There are five swimming pools and three waterslides. It is doubtful that any city anywhere has more water attractions per capita than Medicine Hat. Is it a wonder it is so often described as an oasis?

The largest water slide in southeastern Alberta is well used during the summer.

Cypress Hills

South of Medicine Hat the Buffalo Trail rises and falls over rolling terrain but the net effect is always upward. The coming and going of the glaciers account for these rolls in the landscape. Inching forward, the glaciers plowed the terrain beneath their immense weight. In their melting retreat, they dumped piles of debris and released torrents of water, thus creating and molding hills and dales. But when you arrive on top of the hills, you will find a plateau that is truly flat, for in the most recent period of glaciation, the ice never reached the tops of these hills. The hills were truly an island in the ice.

Island above the Ice

Cypress Hills is Alberta's second largest provincial park (approx. 200 sq. km).

To travel its backroads and to take advantage of its many interpretive opportunities is to learn about a geological history of almost unrivalled uniqueness. The plateau on top of the hills is the highest point of altitude between Banff and Labrador, 500 metres above the surrounding plains. Being higher, the hills are cooler and the prevailing westerly winds, pushed up so suddenly, unleash their moisture in frequent thunderstorms accounting for the Indian name "the Thunder Breeding Hills." This combination of cool and wet makes for a different ecology, and hills sport a strange mixture of prairie and alpine plant varieties.

How the hills came to be this high and to remain so is a complicated story. Millions of years ago, huge rivers poured from the Rocky Mountains and, in this location, those rivers deposited a thick layer of cobble-type stones. Over time, these cobbles were cemented together by sandstone and limestone to form a solid but permeable

A high, solid ridge of conglomerate rock, the tops of the Cypress Hills resisted glaciation.

The cool moist Cypress Hills are a stark contrast to the surrounding arid prairies.

kind of rock called conglomerate. Being hard but also permeable, the conglomerate was more resistant to erosion than the surrounding country. A combination of uplifting and resistance to erosion meant that, over millions of years, the Cypress Hills were left as a high ridge.

When the age of glaciation came, the ice was not deep enough to cover the ridge; the glaciers pushed round it. The Ice Age did affect the hills in other ways, though. Glacial meltwater, trapped between the retreating glaciers and the hills, eventually tore canyons

Fourteen species of orchids are found in the Cypress Hills.

into the ridge on its north and west sides. Also, a sand called *loess*, ground fine by the glaciers, blew onto the hills, and covers them still.

Another unique feature of the Cypress Hills is that two of the major continental watersheds divide here. Water draining from the north slopes finds its eventual way into Hudson's Bay; water shed to the south joins the Missouri-Mississippi system destined for the Gulf of Mexico.

Historically, the Cypress Hills have acted as a dividing line among people. Archaeological digs show signs of human habitation going back 7000 years. But in the period of recorded history, the hills acted as a buffer zone between several Indian tribes. This was also a sacred place for the Indians, who often performed their most important religious ceremony here: the Sun Dance.

The establishment of Cypress Hills Provincial Park in 1952 has done a great deal to restore the hills to the appearance they would have had in the days of the buffalo and the Sun Dance. Tall tussocks of

fescue grass wave on the grass plateau. An elk herd of about 500 grazes the plateau and shelters in the forest perimeters. Some of the other wildlife species you may encounter here are coyote, wild turkey, cottontail rabbit, mule and whitetail deer. Alpine plant species and rare orchid beds tantalize the amateur naturalist.

The crocus is found throughout the prairies.

Horseshoe Canyon and Reesor Lake Viewpoints

The Horseshoe Canyon Viewpoint is a good place to contemplate the height and origin of the hills. You are atop a plateau whose

cap of conglomerate stone resisted erosion for millions of years. If you had stood here during the Ice Age, you would have been surrounded by ice as far as the eye could see. Horseshoe Canyon itself is one part of the scene which has a postglacial origin. When water soaks down into the permeable conglomerate and freezes, it expands and cracks the stone. The cracks grow wider with the years until, finally, a whole area of upland will become unstable and it will slump down. This is how the horseshoe-shaped canyon came to be.

From the Reesor Lake Viewpoint, you can compare the unglaciated terrain of the Cypress Hills plateau to the glaciated landscape beyond the hills. Until it was created by damming in the 1960s, Reesor Lake was two smaller lakes in the Battle Creek valley. The valley is one of those carved by glacial meltwaters trapped between the retreating glacier and the Cypress Hills.

Notice the section of terrain that has broken away. Aspen, spruce and lodgepole pine forest reach for the top of the canyon.

Graburn Monument

The Cypress Hills have had their share of tragic history. Whiskey traders operated posts in the hills during the 1870s and the murder of twenty Assiniboine here by wolf hunters and whiskey traders in 1873 was a major factor leading to the formation of the North-West Mounted Police. The first Mounted Policeman to die violently also met his end in the Cypress Hills. Constable Marmaduke Graburn died here of a bullet wound in 1879 and it was one time that the Mounties did not get their man. A Blood Indian suspect was tried at Fort Macleod in 1881 but the jury acquitted him. A cairn at the eastern end of Cypress Hills park stands in Constable Graburn's memory.

Here and there on the high plateau, a lonely lodgepole pine will grow to maturity without the shade or shelter of others of its kind. One lofty and gnarled landmark of this kind has been dubbed the "Survival Tree."

(Note: the Graburn Monument and the Survival Tree are accessible by gravel road only; travel is not recommended in wet weather.)

Recreational Opportunities

In 1859, explorer John Palliser called the Cypress Hills "an oasis in the desert ... an island in a sea of grass." Like all true oases, the Cypress Hills draws people to it and, in all seasons, visitors are rewarded for making the journey.

The Elkwater community is the area focus, a small town overlooking Elkwater Lake. In summer, the beaches are busy and in all seasons, there are full amenities for the traveller: concession, motel, service station, restaurant, post office, laundromat. Also in town you will find a fine visitor centre with films and displays to guide you in your explorations of the park.

The park's three main water bodies are Elkwater Lake, Reesor Lake and Spruce Coulee Reservoir. Canoes, rowboats, motorized boats and sailboards can be rented in Elkwater. Only non-motorized craft are allowed on Spruce Coulee. Electric motors are allowed on Reesor Lake. There is good fishing in all the lakes. Elkwater is home to yellow perch and northern pike; Reesor Lake is stocked with trout;

The landscape around Ressor Lake is home to mule deer, white-tailed deer, elk, coyote and even wild turkey.

Elkwater Lake allows powered craft but speed limits are in effect within the marina and near swimming areas. Water-skiing, sailing, and windsurfing are popular activities. In the winter, skiing is also popular: the ski hill has a t-bar lift and quad-chairs.

Spruce Coulee is reserved for non-powered leisure boats.

Spruce Coulee has both rainbow and brook trout.

Camping in Cypress Hills is only permitted at the 12 designated camping areas. There are 500 individual campsites and three group camping areas. The facilities range from the basics to full hook-ups.

Cypress Hills is a year-round draw for outdoor enthusiasts. In winter, a ski hill operates here and the back trails are excellent for cross-country skiing. Sites are available for winter camping and fishermen are free to make their winter catches through the ice.

Most places in the world claim to visitors that "there's no place like it." At Cypress Hills, that claim can be made with great conviction. In summer, when the wildflowers bloom through the fescue tufts across the high plateau and, in winter, when the high hills are thick in snow, visitors will feel without having to be told that this is a special place — still an oasis, still an island in the sky.

Beyond Cypress Hills to the U.S. border, the Buffalo Trail winds through a dramatic landscape of lonesome rolling hills: coyote and cowboy country.

North: Where the Buffalo Roamed

Pronghorn antelope, coyotes and rabbits share this vast prairie region. All are timid and extremely fast - the coyote is fast enough to catch a rabbit (sometimes), and the pronghorn can reach speeds of 100 km/hr.

There is a haunting quality to the wide open prairie and a person has not experienced all until he or she has stood alone under the gigantic sky where the land stretches off to the horizon in all directions. This is one of the experiences available to the traveller who takes Highway 41, the Buffalo Trail, north of Medicine Hat. History's travellers to this area spoke of the animal that is no longer here: the buffalo. In 1869, Hudson's Bay Company employee Isaac Cowie passed this way and wrote: ''Our trail fell in with such a herd of buffalo, they looked innumerable. They blackened the whole country.'' Today, this quiet emptiness is home to pronghorn antelope and deer and the sharp-eyed will be able to spot groups of these from the highway.

If the prairies finally make you long for the well-watered valley you left behind, take heart: you meet and cross the South Saskatchewan River again 85 kilometres north of Medicine Hat. Sandy Point Campground at the river crossing is a good place to break your journey.

Empress

The town of Empress, Alberta, is just east of the Buffalo Trail about 32 kilometres north of the Saskatchewan River. Here, the ancient history of this prairie and its modern history stand face to face. On the highest point of land above the town, there are as many as 200 circles of lichen-encrusted rock marking former tipi encampments. Among them is a medicine wheel, a mysterious remnant of Native religion, one of only 25 such wheels in Alberta. Nearby, there are runways leading to an ancient buffalo jump.

Modern history at Empress is exemplified on the Saskatchewan-Alberta border near Empress where Alberta natural gas enters the Trans-Canada Pipeline system destined for eastern Canada. Massive gas processing plants have been built at this spot to strip out gas liquids before the natural gas leaves Alberta.

Oyen

Farther north on the Buffalo Trail, the visitor comes to the town of Oyen, symbolized by the pronghorn antelope. A 75-year-old farmhouse at Oyen has been preserved to commemorate the hardships and the victories of the region's homesteaders. In the house, you will see antique farm implements and the buffalo and bearskin coats the homesteaders wore to survive the savage prairie blizzards. Oyen has a variety of services for the traveller including a campground, a picnic area, a golf course and a swimming pool.

An Intriguing Route

The Buffalo Trail, anchored by its urban centre at Medicine Hat, is an intriguing route. The story that unfolds from what might at first seem to be blank pages is so ancient, so unusual and so rich. There is also a tantalizing amount of history marked out here that cannot be explained: the mystery of the medicine wheel at Empress, the story of how Medicine Hat came to have its name, the mountain plants and rare orchids high in the prairie surrounded by the Cypress Hills. What can be explained is explained through the many interpretive centres and programs available all along the Buffalo Trail. The rest is left to tantalize your imagination when you leave this part of the country and look back on it again and again.

Forty-mile Coulee and Red Rock

If you are approaching the Buffalo Trail on Highway 3 west, consider visiting Forty-mile Coulee south of Bow Island, which has many water-based recreational opportunities.

Red Rock Coulee is approximately 25 km south of Seven Persons off Highway 3.

The Canada goose and mallard duck have made this area one of western Canada's most popular hunting spots.

The
Red Coat
Trail

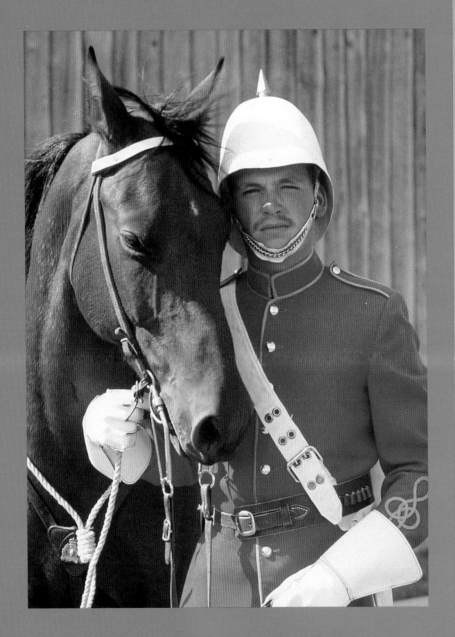

The history of the men in scarlet and gold was written here. Scarcely more than a century into our past, the North-West Mounted Police rode west. Before them lay the prairie, unbroken and unfenced. On this wild frontier, outlaws mixed with whisky traders while Native peoples fought to survive sickness and the demise of the buffalo.

The Mounted Police faced innumerable dangers but in the face of all odds — they endured. Outposts were established, and the law was administered firmly and fairly among the region's scattered inhabitants.

Today, highways traverse this same fertile prairie where the dust from yesterday's conflicts has barely had time to settle. While the grizzlies and buffalo are gone, there are herds of pronghorns, mule deer, whitetail deer and a host of other species in an area of rich faunal diversity. Farming and ranching illustrate the region's agricultural productivity.

There are also many places within this vast land where the rich archaeology from a bygone era manifests itself, where the evidence of early man is "written" on stone and seen in effigies, teepee rings and vision quest sites. Some of the North-West Mounted Police outposts still exist. Others have been reconstructed to capture the excitement and drama from this colourful era.

Milk River

The Milk River Ridge and the Sweet Grass Hills, like Chief Mountain and Crowsnest Mountain to the west, are natural monuments embodying power and intrigue. Soaring more than 1,000 metres (3,281') above the surrounding prairie, the Milk River Ridge is a testimony to the glacial activity that once took place here.

The town of Milk River itself has a unique history compared to other Alberta towns in that at least eight different governments and countries have had jurisdiction over the area. Today, the Canadian flag flies over Milk River but you can stop and see the other seven flags and read their story at the Historical Cairn and Flag Display.

Devil's Coulee Dinosaur Egg Site

It was carved by meltwater at the end of the Ice Age.

The unstable nature of bentonite soils accounts for the intriguing land forms seen here.

From the air it looks like a devil's trident. This is Devil's Coulee, site of one of the earth's most exciting palaeontological discoveries.

Seventy-five million years ago, hadrosaurs (duck-billed dinosaurs) came to lay clutches of eggs in colonial nests. Ten thousand years ago glacial meltwater carved a channel across the Alberta prairie exposing strata from this bygone era. Years passed as snowmelt and rainwater continued to erode the "soft" sandstone. Then, on May 14, 1987, Wendy Sloboda, a 19-year-old student, discovered fossilized egg shell fragments. Today scientists work to remove caches of prehistoric eggs and embryonic bones from ancient nests.

Recovered eggs, approximately 20 cm long, about the size of a large, oblong grapefruit, protect the fetal remains. Hadrosaur hatchlings from the genus *Hypacrosaurus* emerged as chicken-sized animals. Adults weighed as much as 3 tonnes (3,000 kg or 6,600 lbs).

Writing-On-Stone

Travelling east from the town of Milk River, the highway drops into Verdigris Coulee, a glacial meltwater channel, then climbs again to the prairie.

The West Butte of the Sweetgrass Hills draws ever closer, but as the highway turns south to enter Writing-On-Stone Provincial Park, no visitor is ever quite prepared for the scene. Within the blink of an eye, the prairie collapses to reveal a new world of spectacular and

When you canoe downriver, you see the country as the early settlers did one hundred years ago.

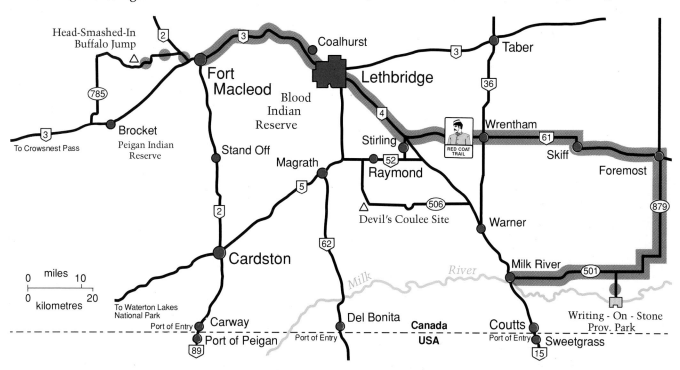

Pictographs are Indian drawings and paintings. Petroglyphs are rock carvings. Both tell of life over two hundred years ago.

Foremost

Prairie elevators are often called "Sentinels of the Plains" and when you drive toward Foremost, you understand why. Towering 200 feet above the flat prairie, these sentinels are a testimony to the entrepreneurial history of Western Canada. Although most grain elevators are made of wood, the Alberta Wheat Pool has built a unique cement elevator called "The Buffalo Slope," which is open to visitors.

From Foremost, turn west on Highway 61 to the junction with Highway 4, and again you are following the trail of the intrepid North-West Mounted Police, as they made their way west to Fort Whoop-Up 100 years ago.

Irrigated agriculture provides a solid business base for Lethbridge.

bizarre sandstone formations. These natural bridges, columns and pinnacles of rock appear in outcrops east and west along the Milk River.

These intricately complex sandstone walls and passageways harbour the largest concentration of pictographs and petroglyphs found on the North American plains. Carved images of men on horseback, shield-bearing warriors, buffalo, bears and bighorn sheep present striking revelations of early habitation, and the powerful sacred attractions of this valley.

The Milk River, a tributary of the Missouri River, serves as home to a number of plant and animal species which are rare or absent to the north. Mule deer and beaver are seen by most visitors and the campground in summer and spring is alive with the songs of countless birds including meadowlarks, eastern and western kingbirds, house wrens, rufous-sided townees and many more.

The Park is also home to a reconstructed North-West Mounted Police outpost. Located at the mouth of Police Coulee, this lonely encampment served to prevent the flow of whisky across the border.

Today, the outpost is quiet. The call of the western meadowlark still speaks of the timelessness of the prairie and allows modern visitors to contemplate the sobering dimensions of the past.

In addition to being an important water source in this arid region, the Milk River provides a variety of recreational opportunities. The picturesque waterway affords canoeists adventure and vistas of wildlife (including nesting golden eagles, prairie falcons and ferruginous hawks) amid a landscape touched and revered by early man.

Lethbridge

Like the spokes of a giant wheel, the highways into Lethbridge draw the people of southwestern Alberta into their urban hub. Lethbridge is the centre of a remarkably broad trading region and on any day you can see in the city the many colourful strands that make

Park Place Shopping Centre

up the weave of life in southwestern Alberta. On the broad streets of the city mingle farmers, ranchers, Native people, Hutterites and cowboys: the atmosphere is a mix of business and holiday as deals are made and old acquaintances renewed.

Lethbridge has been such a crossroads and centre of trade since the 1860s. From 1869 to 1874, when the fur trade involved a great deal of whisky, the traders came north by wagon and cart from Fort Benton, Montana. Their main destination was Fort Whoop-Up, near where Lethbridge stands today. After the North-West Mounted Police came west in 1874 to stop the trade of whisky, the stream of commerce along the Whoop-Up Trail adapted; the bull teams hauled provisions for the Mounties. Later, they would supply the needs of the area's first settlers.

Serving its region is a tradition of long standing in Lethbridge. Adopting the motto "*Everything under the Sun*," Lethbridge (pop: 60,000) has more hotels, motels, shopping areas and entertainment opportunities than you would expect in a city of its size. The network of natural areas and historic sites in the Oldman River valley express appreciation for both the land and its history.

The sharp-tailed grouse is usually found near shrubbery or grass thicket but occasionally will perch on a fence.

History Within the City Limits

An ideal place to begin to look at the historic side of Lethbridge is the Sir Alexander Galt Museum: named for a former Canadian High Commissioner. The Galt Museum is at the western end of Fifth Avenue South, just above the Oldman River valley escarpment. Four galleries in the museum tell the human history of Lethbridge and area, and windows along the west side of the building allow a panoramic view of the valley.

This view gives a quick orientation to the region's history. The section of valley on the near side of the river is Indian Battle Park, commemorating the site of the 1870 conflict between the Blackfoot and their traditional enemies the Plains Cree. Though the Cree won the initial battle, the Blood were soon reinforced by their Peigan allies and, in a decisive battle at the site of Indian Battle Park, the Cree were solidly defeated. The Blackfoot victory was largely due to the leadership of the Métis scout Jerry Potts.

Directly below the museum, again on the near side of the river, you will

The High Level Bridge is 96 metres high and 1623 metres long.

see a rectangular wooden palisade. This is a replica of the notorious whisky trading establishment Fort Whoop-Up.

Fort Whoop-Up was the most important of 44 southern Alberta whisky forts and it was the main target of the North-West Mounted Police when they marched west to clean up the whisky trade in 1874. When you take a closer look at Fort Whoop-Up, you will see that the trade took place through a barred grate in the fort's outer wall. Rifles were trained on the Indians through loopholes. You will also see the original 1869 cannon with which the traders defended their fort.

Colonel James Macleod was in charge of the force

of Mounties that marched on Fort Whoop-Up in the fall of 1874, under the guidance of Jerry Potts. Potts knew Fort Whoop-Up well having worked there as a hunter. He had grown disgusted with the whisky trade and was willing to help the Mounties put an end to it. But word of the Mounties' approach had preceded them to Fort Whoop-Up and the heavily armed force met no resistance. The fort was empty save for one old man who met them cordially.

At Fort Whoop-Up you will see various displays and a fifteen minute audiovisual presentation. The Whoop-Up flag that flew over the fort in its heyday is the official flag of Lethbridge. Note its resemblance to the American flag, due to

the influence of the early American whisky traders.

Another attraction inside Indian Battle Park is a "medicine stone." The Blood Indians believed this reddish boulder had sacred significance to the Blood Indians and for many years they left offerings on it.

The next image we turn to is the one that probably caught your attention first: the High Level railway bridge spanning the valley from cliff to cliff atop its high black trestle. The kilometre long, 96 metre high bridge is an impressive sight by any standard: one of the most photographed structures in Western Canada. The bridge was built as a result of the CPR decision in 1905

The museum houses over 130,000 original items.

to move its Division Point on the Crowsnest Pass line from Fort Macleod to Lethbridge. By this decision Lethbridge became the main market, distribution and service centre for the region. It has a lot to do with why Lethbridge is a city today.

Before you leave your viewpoint, have a good look at another far more recent highlight. Built into the ravines of the opposite side of the valley is the University of Lethbridge. Famed Canadian architect

The establishment of Fort Whoop-Up and other whisky forts was a primary reason for the federal government to establish the North-West Mounted Police.

Arthur Erikson designed the university to blend with both the banks of the valley and the prairie upland.

These sites merit a closer look and the access roads are all handy to the Sir Alexander Galt Museum.

Parks and Gardens

One of the many unique aspects of Lethbridge is that it is built beside rather than in the Oldman River valley. The largely undisturbed valley has been turned into a series of parks and nature reserves.

Two greenspaces stand adjacent to Indian Battle Park: a nature reserve downriver and Botterill Bottom Park upriver (on the other side of Whoop-Up Drive). On the opposite side of the river is Bull Trail Park.

A few kilometres downriver are Pavan Park and the Alexander Wilderness Park. All these river valley parks contain well developed paths for hiking, and all but the latter are part of the 28 km Coal Banks Trail system for cycling.

If the river valley parks are symbols of nature's accomplishment, Henderson Park off Mayor Magrath Drive is a grand illustration of what human beings can accomplish in

harmony with nature. Henderson Lake is a large artificial lake ringed by mature trees and encircled by a pathway. The surrounding park contains a bowling green, a swimming pool, a shoreline pavilion and boat rental, and picnic shelters. Just outside the park, across the roadways ringing it, are a variety of other recreational facilities: the Ice Centre, Henderson Stadium, tennis courts, the Henderson Campground and Whoop-Up Park (home of the annual Whoop-Up Days Exhibition and Stampede).

But the pièce de résistance of Henderson Park is without doubt the Nikka

Terraces are part of the Coal Banks Trail System, linking facilities and parks in Lethbridge.

The Brewery Gardens and Tourist Information Centre greet you as you enter Lethbridge from Highway 3 west.

The Henderson Lake area is a centre of recreational activity in Lethbridge.

Yuko Centennial Garden, a precisely authentic Japanese landscape garden. The venerable tradition of the Japanese garden is to create a place of peace and meditation, and to walk along the curved paths and among the rock gardens and reflecting pools of Nikka Yuko is to feel almost instant relief from the stresses of the world.

The wish to build a Japanese garden in Lethbridge came in part from the local Japanese-Canadian community and partly from the rest of the community, wanting to show respect for the Japanese-Canadian contribution to southern Alberta.

One more garden of interest is the Brewery Garden found near the east end of the High Level

Bridge. This ornamental garden on the steep slope of a ravine is one of Lethbridge's oldest attractions, developed as a courtesy by the brewery. There is a Tourist Information Centre on site.

Lethbridge: Other Attractions

Lethbridge has a great deal more to interest and entertain its visitors. On Highway 3 just east of the city is the Lethbridge Agriculture Centre which combines the research facilities of both Agriculture Canada and Alberta Agriculture. This is the largest of Canada's 37 federal agricultural research stations. It has been coming up with scientific solutions to agricultural problems since the turn of the century.

The Southern Alberta Art Gallery is located on the south side of Galt Gardens, a park in the heart of downtown. The gallery features exhibitions by local, national and international artists.

Also downtown is the Bowman Arts Centre at 9th Street and 4th Avenue South, a community arts centre featuring the work of local and regional artists. It is open year round from 10 A.M. to 10 P.M., Monday through Friday.

The Japanese Garden is an interpretation and artistic arrangement of natural elements which bring peace and appreciation to the viewer.

Towards Fort Macleod

When you leave Lethbridge, headed west along Highway 3, you are following the path the North-West Mounted Police took after their surprisingly easy conquest of Fort Whoop-Up. It was by now late fall of 1874. As you drive you can imagine the already-white mountains growing ever larger before the North-West Mounted Police cavalcade, the partially frozen Oldman River winding in its valley beside them. The pitched battle with the outlaw whisky traders having failed to materialize, all thoughts would have been on winter food and shelter.

This Red Coat Trail sign can be seen along Highways 3, 4 and 61 as a guide for travellers seeking to share the experience of the first North-West Mounted Police

Blood Indian Reservation

On the south side of Highway #3, extending as far as the eye can see, is the Blood Indian Reservation, at 1047 square kilometres the largest Indian reservation in Canada. The reserve once boasted the largest wheatfield in the British Commonwealth. Today, in addition to farming and ranching, the Blood tribe has added a variety of businesses to its economic base, including the manufacturing of modular constructed homes at the huge Kainai Industries plant. The public is invited to tour the plant. (Please telephone ahead of time: 1-800-661-8031).

Fort Macleod

Fifty-two kilometres west of Lethbridge you will arrive at the town of Fort Macleod. In 1874, Jerry Potts recommended this low-banked well-wooded stretch of valley to Colonel Macleod

The sandstone buildings were originally erected as a protection against fire.

With their scarlet dress tunics, the North-West Mounted Police were known as "Red Coats." Their original force numbered three hundred and was led by Commissioner G.A. French. Fort Macleod (below) was the first of many North-West Mounted Police forts established in the West.

as a site for his winter fort. The first Fort Macleod was built on an island in the river. Spring flooding prompted a move to higher ground in 1883.

Fort Macleod is southern Alberta's oldest settlement and the number of buildings retained from its early days led the Alberta government to designate the downtown core a Provincial Historic Area. Practically every building along Main Street has a story to tell and both guided and self-guided walking tours are available.

Here are a few of the historic highlights you will find along that tour.

A block south of Main Street, the offices of the Town of Fort Macleod are

in a stately brick building. Built in 1902 this was originally a territorial court house. Colonel James Macleod, in addition to his Mounted Police duties, had been the local magistrate and was by this time Territorial Supreme Court Judge in Southern Alberta.

The present home of the *Macleod Gazette* on Main Street was, in 1906, the Kennefick Livery. The *Gazette* is one of the oldest newspapers in Alberta and its back issues tell the colourful story of the West. An 1882 entry tells of an unfortunate Mr. Bowles who was "lynched by some cowboys on the Indian Basin. He refused to assist them to fight a prairie fire and, after the boys got it out, they went to the creek where he was camped, took him and hung him."

If you drop in on Main Street's Midnight News and Novelty, you will be in one of the oldest businesses in town: the building dates back to 1890.

Across Main Street, you will see the marquee of the Empress Theatre (1912), once a vaudeville stage. It now has a summer theatre featuring historical musical comedies.

This is indeed rich territory for anyone with an interest in southern Alberta's past: a modern town thriving within the brick walls and behind the false fronts of another era.

Head-Smashed-In was used by the Indians as a "jump" from at least 3600 B.C., more than five centuries before the building of pyramids of Egypt. The Porcupine Hills are in the background.

Pow-wows draw Native people from across Western Canada and the Northern United States.

Fort Museum

Undoubtedly the biggest single attraction in the town of Fort Macleod is the Fort Museum, a reconstruction of the Mounted Police fort brimming with artifacts and documents of the region's past. Children love to walk the palisades and to peek out through the loopholes in the corner bastions. Adults will find equal pleasure in the attractively presented historical displays. A special summer attraction in the fort's parade ground is the

Mounted Police Musical Ride, performed by riders in traditional Mounted Police uniform. The fort contains the original Fred Kanouse house, on its original site. Kanouse was a 19th century fur trader who operated a number of posts in southern Alberta, teaming up at one point with famous Waterton Lakes National Park pioneer, Kootenai Brown. Also reconstructed on its original site is the law office and living quarters of F.W.G. Haultain, the first practising lawyer in Fort Macleod. Haultain went on to become, in 1897, the Premier of the North-West Territories.

The Fort Museum is truly one of the finest museums in all Western Canada.

Head-Smashed-In Buffalo Jump

Though not a part of the Red Coat Trail, the Head-Smashed-In Buffalo Jump makes a grand finale to this journey. Just 20 kilometres west of Fort Macleod on Secondary Highway 785, Head-Smashed-In has an interpretive centre and an archaeological site where the story of 5500 years of human activity is being unearthed and explained. The mystery of how a relatively small number of Indians, working on foot, could induce huge herds of buffalo to stampede over these sandstone cliffs to their deaths is one with which the finest archaeological minds in the world have grappled, and grapple

still. The fruit of that research is available to the visitor in breath-taking displays.

Head-Smashed-In is a UNESCO World Heritage Site. Only seven sites in Canada have been placed on that select list. The site is a reminder that, as important as the whisky trade and the coming of the Mounted Police may have been to 19th century Western Canada, these events are relatively recent and short-term. Hundreds of generations of Native people preceded the white man here, a story of endurance at which we of the 20th century must marvel and admire.

Visitors may watch as archaeologists slowly and carefully continue to unwrap the mysteries of the buffalo jump.

The interpretive centre has many interesting displays and educational programs for visitors of all ages.

Market Garden Tour

*T*he seamless blue sky stretches to meet the land. Here the summer sunlight seems thicker as it pours down, encouraging the crops. This area was once covered in a vast shallow glacial lake, meltwater from the Laurentide Glacier, the last great ice sheet to cover North America. As the glacier receded farther, the lake drained, and the lake bed was transformed into nutrient-rich top soil.

This area has a wider diversity of crops than any other part of the province, so take advantage of the roadside stands and farmers' markets overflowing with fresh produce.

Crops grow best with plenty of sunshine, a moderate climate and ample precipitation. Although the farmland you will see on the Market Garden Tour is blessed with constantly sunny skies and weather moderated by warm Chinook winds, it is desperately short of water. Irrigation has had an almost miraculous effect on the area's agricultural industry. Farms that would normally produce only hay and grain now grow alfalfa, sugar beets and market vegetables, including the best sweet corn in the West.

While contributing to the local economy, irrigation also provides recreation. Man-made reservoirs are used for all kinds of water sports, making the Taber area a place for fun as well as fresh food. This is indeed the ''Land of Plenty Under the Lo-o-o-ng Sun.''

Lethbridge and Taber

Lethbridge

Lethbridge is surrounded by farm land, so it is not surprising that the city is a growing concern. Included in the Market Garden tour are two unique gardens and an agricultural research centre.

At the Agriculture Canada Research Centre, located on Highway 3 at the east entrance of the city, the focus is on dry-land agriculture in greenhouses and test plots, where scientists are constantly striving to improve the hybrid varieties of crops so farmers can make the most of the land.

Corn harvesting west of Taber

Located near the west entrance to the city by the High Level bridge are the spectacular Lethbridge (Molson) Brewery Gardens. Looking at the thousands of brilliantly coloured flowering plants, it is hard to believe that the area was originally a dump for the coal ashes from the adjacent brewery.

Another remarkable spot in Lethbridge is the site of the Nikka Yuko Japanese

Agriculture Canada plays a significant research role in crop development.

Gardens, just off Mayor Magrath Drive, toward Henderson Lake. This beautiful and serene garden is authentic in all detail, from the lichened stone lanterns to the ritual of the tea ceremony which is performed in the pavilion. In fact, it is the only authentic Japanese garden in Canada.

For more information on the many other attractions of this city, please refer to the Red Coat Trail.

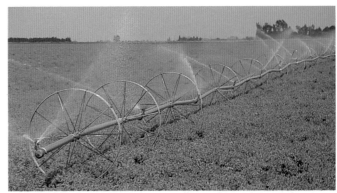

Irrigated field on Highway 3 near Chin. Irrigation is the key to economic growth in the area.

Stafford and Chin Lakes

This irrigation reservoir provides a cooling break on a hot day. The day-use area provides opportunities for swimming, boating, and some terrific wind surfing.

Chin hamlet was once named Woodpecker in reference to a nearby island in the Oldman River. The hamlet is now named for Chin Coulee, the formation that extends south and east of the highway for 50 kilometres. When the Laurentide Glacier receded, the meltwater carved deep drainage channels — or coulees — as it flowed into the river valleys.

When you pass Chin, three igloo-like structures dominate the view. They are massive storage facilities for local produce.

Barnwell

The first settlers came to the Barnwell area in 1903 and constructed a reservoir, dam and ditches that provided water for homes, gardens, livestock, crops, and even strawberries and plum trees. The system was operated and maintained by those who benefitted from the water, and its success set a precedent for future co-operative irrigation projects.

Taber and Area

Taber

If you stand quietly in the gentle warmth of a July evening, you can almost hear the rustle of the corn stalks as they grow ever taller. Jubilee, Super Sweet and Sugar Buns are just a few of the varieties of corn grown around Taber. The ideal combination of sun and soil has made the name of the town synonymous with perfect sweet corn. The season lasts from early August through to early September as different varieties reach their peaks. The Taber Cornfest celebrates this special crop with two days of fun, games and,

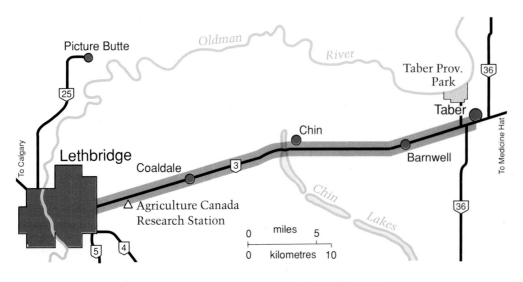

Take advantage of the many roadside farmers' markets

of course, corn tasting.

Corn is just one of the many vegetable crops that thrive here. Almost 40% of Alberta-grown vegetables for sale in local supermarkets are grown on 600 hectares of land around Taber, and that does not include the thousand of hectares of potato crops. The only two vegetable processing plants in Alberta are located in Lethbridge and Taber, and an additional 1640 hectares of land supply produce to these plants.

Empress Foods processes fruits and vegetables such as corn, bean and squash in its Taber plant, and markets its products throughout the West.

The sugar that sweetened your morning coffee probably came from sugar beets grown locally and processed in Taber by the Alberta Sugar Company. Here the huge white root of the sugar beet yields an astonishing 35 teaspoons of sugar.

The irrigation system that brings water to the fields also brings water to the

greens and fairways of Taber's 18-hole golf course. After all that corn, you may want to play a round of golf.

Just north of town, along the banks of the Oldman River, the provincial park provides a more natural recreation area. It is also an ideal area to spot a few of the over 250 species of birds.

Taber corn is highly regarded in Western Canada.

Ethnic Diversity

Among the first settlers here were a handful of industrious Mormons from Utah and Idaho who arrived in 1903 by covered wagon. Having negotiated land and cash in exchange for building a canal system for the Alberta Railway and Irrigation Company, Mormon leader Charles Card called fellow church members to assist in the project.

Potato harvesting at Taber plant

Fourteen years later, another religious group found refuge in Southern Alberta. The print head scarves and long dark skirts of the Hutterite women and the black denim suits of the Hutterite men have not changed in style since the first members of this German-speaking Christian sect first arrived from the United States in 1918. Their communal farms have thrived and the fruits (and vegetables) of their labours are available for sale at the local farmers' markets.

It was also during this period that the Scots and the British began their waves of migration. Knowledgeable and skillful miners, they opened the first coal mines in the area.

People of many nationalities from Central Europe came to Southern Alberta in search of freedom and a new life, and hard work and a knowledge of the land allowed them to prosper here.

The area's cultural diversity was further enhanced during WW II, when the federal government evacuated all Japanese Canadians from the Pacific Coast. Most of the Japanese re-settled in central British Columbia,

but some were brought to southern Alberta. When restrictions were lifted six years after their arrival, many stayed and today have successful farms and businesses.

In the early 1950s the industrious Dutch first settled here, and since that time their culture has also enriched the area.

A Hutterite colony near Taber

The Lo-o-ong Sun

The sky that seems to stretch forever, the irrigation that gives life to the soil and the crops that produce food for export around the world combine to create a most unusual tour on this little stretch of highway between Lethbridge and Taber.

Mechanization has significantly improved the economics of harvesting corn.

Waterton Lakes Heritage Tour

*O*f all the towering ramparts and soaring cloud-hung buttresses that make up the western skyline of southwestern Alberta, one peak stands alone. It rises in Montana, set apart from the front range of the Rockies, and casts a long shadow over the extreme southwestern corner of Alberta. It catches the eye of every visitor to Lethbridge, Fort Macleod, Cardston or Pincher Creek. It towers over the boundary line between Canada and the United States, and over the divided reservations of the Blackfoot, who once roamed as a united nation at its foot.

They called it Chief Mountain, and it is still a sacred altar to the Blackfoot, who have always dwelled within sight of it. On its bluffs are the lichen-covered remains of vision quest sites, where warriors went to fast and pray for a spirit helper to make them powerful at war and in the hunt. This great block of soaring rock is the home of Thunder, an imperious and demanding spirit who shares its forbidding precipices with an equally imposing being, West Wind.

Visible from the junction of Highways 3 west and 6 south, Chief Mountain is the southern landmark for motorists bound for Pincher Creek and Waterton Lakes National Park. Along the way, you will find an abundance of wildlife, historic points of interest, striking vistas where mountain and prairies meet, and pleasant spots to pause and picnic.

Pincher Creek

Waterton International Heritage Tour begins at the junction of Highway 3 and Highway 6 south. Follow Highway 6 about 5 km to Pincher Creek, a small ranching community nestled along a stream bottom. Here, you will find the Kootenai Brown

The town of Pincher Creek overlooks the prairies to the east and the foothills and mountains to the west.

Museum and the Lebel Mansion. The museum tells the story of the pioneers in the rough old days of the West.

On the museum ground is the cabin of Kootenai Brown, the first white resident of nearby Waterton Lakes National Park, whose spirit symbolizes the hardy nature of the newcomers to this wild land.

British army officer, Pony Express rider, warrior, and loving husband to a native wife: Kootenai was all of these and much more, toughened by the times he lived in. During one altercation, he received an arrow in the back that just missed the kidneys. "I thought my time had come," he recalled. "The jagged edges caught the flesh as I pulled it out, and gave me great pain. I had a bottle of turpentine, and opening up the wound, one of my companions inverted the bottle and when I bent over, about half a pint ran into the opening." On the empty plains of Alberta, weaklings did not survive.

Kootenai was also a homespun thinker and conservationist. Waterton Lakes National Park owes its origins to conversations at Kootenai's cabin between Brown and Alberta pioneer and local rancher F.W Godsal. As the result of a

Kootenai Brown first operated a trading post in the area and later became park guardian. He died in 1917.

letter from Godsal, the federal government set aside the nucleus of Waterton Park as a forest reserve in 1895. Brown was the first park superintendent, retiring at the age of seventy-five. His grave at Waterton is a fitting resting place for a mountain man who believed in giving something back to the generous land.

Continuing on Highway 6, south of Pincher Creek, the road seems an arbitrary divider between the cultivated fields to the east and the unbroken ranchlands to the west. Groves of trembling aspen and meadows of rough fescue sweep west to the foot of the Rockies, where pasture gives way to slopes covered in pine and spruce.

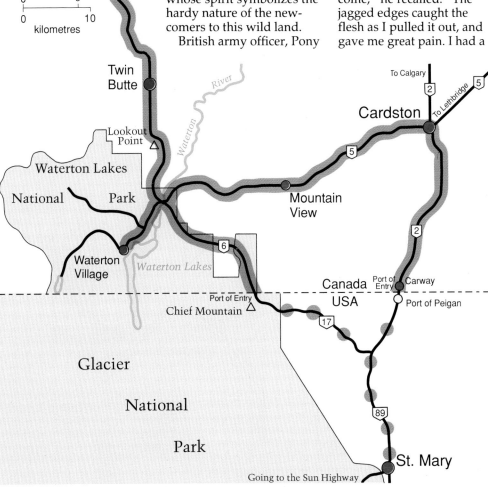

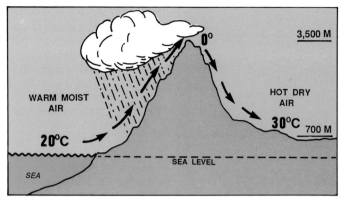

Wind of the west: compression of downward moving air raises a Chinook wind's temperature.

The Wind of the West

Does the car suddenly seem to lack power as you approach the mountains? Has it begun to rock back and forth on its beam like a child's sailboat on a duck pond? Don't be alarmed; it's not an earthquake. It's the West Wind, or Chinook as it is also known. It shapes the prairie, giving contour to the hills and shifting the top-soil during dry periods. It is the wind that overpowered the trees and made a home instead for the grass that deer, elk and cattle graze on.

The people here have a saying, "If you don't like the weather now, wait an hour for it to change." This is no exaggeration. Between midnight and 1 A.M. on January 27, 1962, the legendary Chinook wind raised the temperature at Pincher Creek from -20°F to +37°F, a change of 57 degrees in one hour. This warm wind, accompanied by the "Chinook Arch" of clouds, is caused by Pacific air masses which lose their moisture on the west side of the Great Divide and are heated in their rapid descent of the "East Slope" the ranges you see to the west.

Twin Butte

Two low lying hills, one on each side of the road, mark the hamlet of Twin Butte. The old community hall recalls an era of horses stamping their feet in the snow, while fiddle music and laughter broke the stillness of a winter night. There is a strong sense of community here still among these far flung ranches, and with it goes a love of the land which adds its own beauty to this drive.

Pine Ridge

Soon the highway curves and begins to descend to Pine Ridge, where a fine overlook invites you to stop. From here you see Waterton Lakes National Park, a Biosphere Reserve which is part of the United Nations' Man and the Biosphere Programme. The reserve includes the protected lands of the national park, as well as lands around it which have been modified by humans. This creates an opportunity to better manage resources, since the effects of land use around the undeveloped land can be scientifically compared to use in the natural area of the reserve. Government agencies, ranchers, oil executives and others meet to discuss and resolve conservation issues that affect the area, with the knowledge that they are dealing with a resource that is internationally significant.

Also this is Andy Russell country. Former outfitter and guide, Russell is one of Canada's better known authors and conservationists. It is not hard to see how such books as *Grizzly Country* and *The Rockies* might have been inspired by such an astounding landscape.

Bison Enclosure and Prairie Life Zone

Nearing the park boundary, you will encounter a fenced herd of buffalo. This is part of Waterton's Prairie Life Zone and marks the western limit of the prairie that stretches from Alberta to Manitoba.

Bison paddock, north of Waterton Lakes National Park.

Bear Grass has a spectacular torch-like flowering stalk composed of hundreds of small cream coloured flowers. The tough leaves were used by natives for making baskets and the roots were steeped and used as a hair tonic.

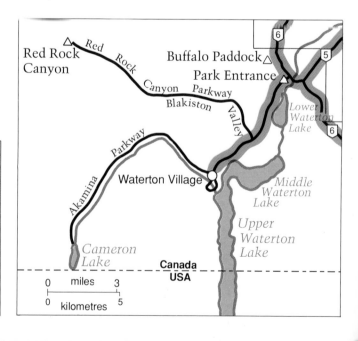

Waterton Lakes National Park

No matter what the season, Waterton Lakes National Park has some of the most spectacular opportunities for viewing wildlife of any national park in Canada. You may see scattered bands of elk, as well as mule deer and white-tailed deer, moose, bighorn sheep, and mountain goats, whose shaggy white coats and jet black horns distinguish them from the tawny-coloured ewes of the bighorn. Bighorn rams are identified by their massive horns which curve upward. You may occasionally see black and grizzly bears. Please give them a wide berth.

Waterton is the starting point of a continental trail system which goes all the way to the Mexican border. Throughout Waterton, you'll find many hiking trails, some leading across the border to Glacier National Park. Overall, Waterton-Glacier International Peace Park offers over 1280 km of backcountry hiking trails with varying terrain.

Waterton Lakes

In the shadow of the mountains lie Waterton Lakes, created during the last ice age — which ended only 10,000 years ago — by a gigantic valley glacier, and their formation was similar to that of the fjords of British Columbia and Norway. The water that fills the lakes today begins as American glacial ice on mountains in Glacier National Park, Montana.

At 148 metres, Waterton Lake, the deepest lake in the

The most widely spread member of the deer family in Alberta, mule deer are named for their large ears.

The mountain goat's stocky legs keep the body's centre of gravity low while the small, oval hooves contain spongy pads which act like suction cups.

Rockies, is the home of exotic species like the opossum shrimp, which "plays possum" when the pigmy whitefish and the deepwater sculpin come swimming by.

Middle Waterton Lake is slowly disappearing. Gravel and silt washed down the mountains by Blakiston Creek are collecting in the delta, and in a few thousand years, the lake will no longer exist.

Red Rock Canyon Parkway

Follow the course of Blakiston Creek up the Red Rock Canyon Parkway. This 16 km side trip should not be missed. One of two scenic parkways in the area, it is a favoured location for viewing the Waterton wildlife. Many of the animals seem tame, but they are wild and should be treated as such.

Along the parkway there are picnic grounds, a major campground and several popular hiking trails. At the end is a short nature walk (1 km), where red argillite rocks and crystalline pools of mountain water delight the eye.

This valley was the route taken by generations of Kootenay tribes on their way from B.C. to hunt buffalo on the plains. Their ancestors camped along Waterton Lakes for thousands of years before the coming of the whites.

Here, as part of the

Palliser Expedition of September, 1857, came Lt. Thomas Blakiston, his moccasins still wet from a snowy crossing of the South Kootenay Pass. He named the Waterton Lakes after a renowned British naturalist, Charles Waterton, and the highest mountain (2893 m) after himself.

The Prince of Wales Hotel

Returning to the main park highway, continue south. Before you, on a promontory overlooking the lake, is the Prince of Wales Hotel, one of southern Alberta's most beautiful buildings. During its construction in 1927, the frame was struck by a powerful gale. To this day it remains slightly out

Most visitors to the Red Rock Canyon will attest to the fact that in nine out of ten visits they will encounter wildlife near the road.

Cameron Falls, located in downtown Waterton, is a popular spot for photographers.

of plumb, in homage to West Wind's power.

From the front of the hotel, the view is a magnificent panorama that stretches right down into Montana at the far end of the lake. You are looking at part of Glacier National Park, which is the American half of Waterton-Glacier International Peace Park. The idea for this symbolic gesture of international good will was put forward by the Rotary Club of North America, and the Peace Park was dedicated by President Hoover in 1932. Below your vantage point, the picturesque town of Waterton lies on the delta formed from the outwash of Cameron Creek.

Opposite the hotel, on the west side of the main park road, the park information centre is a vital stop for every visitor.

The Village of Waterton

Village shopping

Waterton village nestles in the heart of Waterton Lakes National Park. Not to be missed during a visit to the town is the internationally-acclaimed Cameron Falls. Go straight down Evergreen Avenue, then right at the stop sign. Before you, Cameron Creek spills down. This is a "hanging valley": the main Waterton glacier carved its way through the billion-year-old limestone, lowered the main valley, and left Cameron Creek hanging in a perpetual rainbow.

Back along its main street, Waterton has shops to provide for all the needs of its visitors. Visitor services include accommodation, shopping, golfing, horseback riding, hiking, camping, and recreational water activities such as windsurfing and swimming.

At the village marina, scenic boat cruises take visitors up Waterton Lake across the international boundary to Goat Haunt, Montana, a remote ranger station.

In addition, there are numerous informative interpretive programs including guided walks, theatre programs and exhibits.

The Akamina Parkway

One of the most beautiful drives in Waterton follows the valley of Cameron Creek to Cameron Lakes via the Akamina Parkway. Along the way are picnic grounds and the site of Oil City, where Alberta's first oil well was drilled in 1902.

When you reach Ameron Lake, you can do something very unusual: you can rent a canoe and paddle into the United States

Winds reach speeds of up to 70 km per hour.

under the brooding shadow of Mount Custer at the south end of the lake. Up above on the avalanche slopes, you may be fortunate enough to see a grizzly bear: one with dual citizenship, since grizzly bears don't read maps.

A Royal Canadian Mounted Police constable, with the Prince of Wales Hotel in the background.

Ferry tours are conducted throughout Waterton Lakes.

The area around Waterton Lakes offers a variety of high country hiking trails for the amateur and advanced hiker.

South to Chief Mountain

If you would rather drive than paddle into the U.S., return to the park entrance and follow Highway 6, the Chief Mountain international highway, south to Glacier Park, Montana. The road takes you to within shouting distance of the mountain.

Stop first at the scenic overlook to the Waterton Valley 8 kilometres south of the park entrance. Here, there is a panorama of mountains in the midst of change. Water is cutting "V" shaped valleys down their sides, carrying gravel and dissolved limestone downstream, diminishing these giants bit by bit. Ice forms in crevices and slowly pries the rock apart; gravity carries the debris to the base of the cliffs to form scree and talus slopes. Trees slowly seed themselves in the barren rock and inch their ways up the mountains in a long process of change.

Chief Mountain is to the west as we swing back north on U.S. 89, following the route of Blackfoot warriors who often came this way long ago.

Cardston

Return to Canada, and follow Highway 2 north to Cardston.

In 1887, Charles Ora Card led a wagon train of 42 Mormon immigrants from Utah to found the town which bears his name. Here, settlers began the first irrigation systems in Alberta, precursors of the huge industry which today forms the economic base of southern Alberta.

The Remington-Alberta Carriage Collection features more than 50 antique carriages ranging from stagecoach and buckboard through barouche and formal sleigh. The landau has been used by Queen Elizabeth II during state visits to Alberta and for the opening ceremonies of the Calgary Winter Olympics. Pending completion of the new $11 million carriage centre being built by the Province of Alberta, the collection is temporarily on display in the skating rink (behind the Card log home)

Mormon Temple, Cardston

Remington - Alberta Carriage Collection

for four months every summer.

The building for which Cardston is most famous, the Mormon Temple, cannot be missed, because it can be seen from every point in town.

One of the most beloved buildings in town is the original Card homestead. To step into this cabin is to step back 100 years: a lady's comb on a sideboard, a well-thumbed Bible on the table, give an immediate connection to the pioneer's life and habits, and put flesh on the ghosts of the past.

Visit the Cobblestone Manor, the labour of love of Henry Hoet, a Belgian immigrant. He added 200 tons of cobblestones, gathered by hand from Lee's Creek, to an existing long building in order to create the Manor. The Cobblestone Manor is now a restaurant.

The Courthouse museum, our first provincial courthouse, has an interesting feature: a turn of the century hoosegow in the basement, where the guide will be quite happy to lock you up for a few minutes so you can ponder your sins.

Coming Full Circle

As we turn west on Highway 5, Chief Mountain, standing out from the "shining mountains" of the Blackfoot, points our way back to Pincher Creek. These rolling hills, ranches nestled at their feet, were left as monuments by the great Laurentide Ice Sheet that once covered an area from Hudson's Bay to the Rocky Mountains.

Don't miss the Caribou Clothing Store at Mountain View, which is a sheepskin manufacturing outlet with a crafts store.

Campgrounds and picnic sites will be found on the next stretch of highway.

Now the hills are gentler, setting the stage for the Lewis Range that once again greets us with its sudden, dominating uplift from the plain. There is time for a final look at the massive altar of the West Wind before we come to the junction with Highway 6 where, having come full circle, our tour concludes.

Chief Mountain

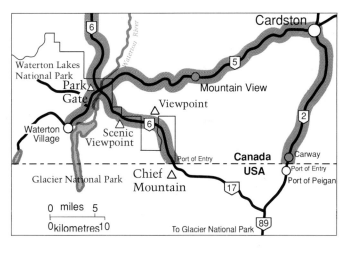

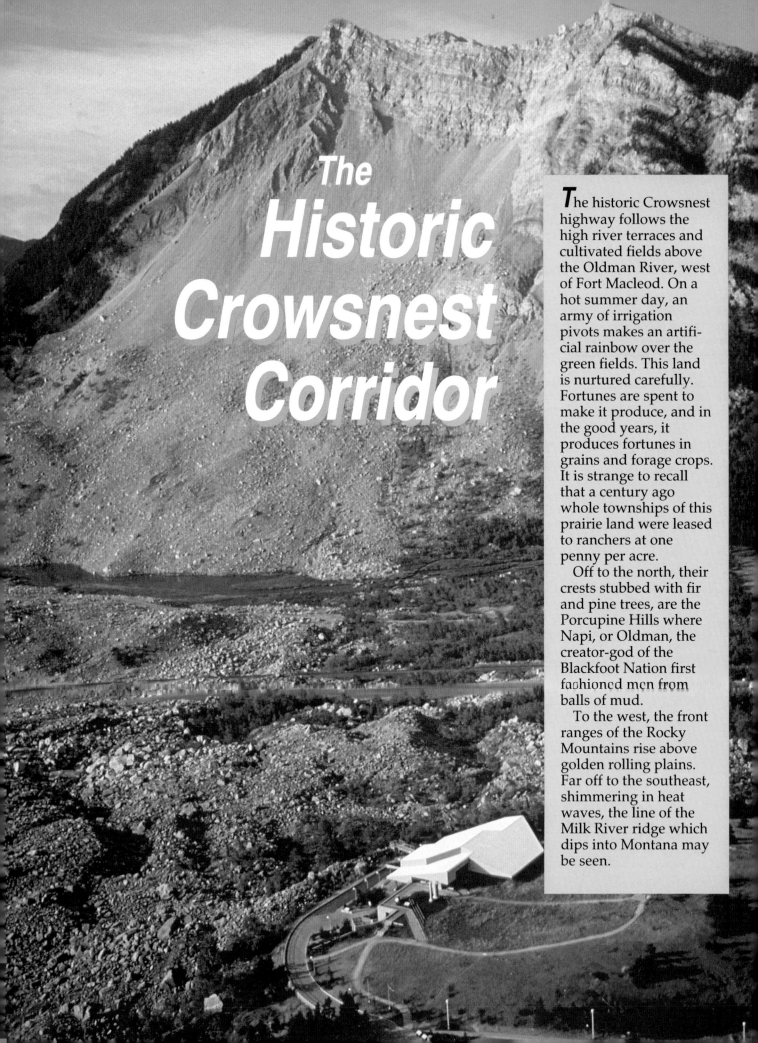

The Historic Crowsnest Corridor

The historic Crowsnest highway follows the high river terraces and cultivated fields above the Oldman River, west of Fort Macleod. On a hot summer day, an army of irrigation pivots makes an artificial rainbow over the green fields. This land is nurtured carefully. Fortunes are spent to make it produce, and in the good years, it produces fortunes in grains and forage crops. It is strange to recall that a century ago whole townships of this prairie land were leased to ranchers at one penny per acre.

Off to the north, their crests stubbed with fir and pine trees, are the Porcupine Hills where Napi, or Oldman, the creator-god of the Blackfoot Nation first fashioned men from balls of mud.

To the west, the front ranges of the Rocky Mountains rise above golden rolling plains. Far off to the southeast, shimmering in heat waves, the line of the Milk River ridge which dips into Montana may be seen.

Nearing the Pass

History

The history of settlement in this part of Alberta is just a bit more than an old man's life span. The Blackfoot shaped Alberta's history by confining trading and early settlement north of the North Saskatchewan. Up until 1877, when the Blackfoot signed Treaty No.

7, they were known as fierce fighters, and most white travellers gave their country a wide berth.

The town of Brocket, headquarters of the Peigan tribe, reminds the traveller that this is still Blackfoot country. Today, the Peigan or Pikuni live between the towns of Fort Macleod and Pincher Creek. There is a growing movement among these people to keep alive their language and religious beliefs. Here, there is a small trading post where the art and craftsmanship of the Peigan can be seen at first hand.

Highway 3 leads you into the historic Crowsnest Pass on your way to Crowsnest Mountain.

Lundbreck Falls

The Crowsnest Pass itself has been explored by generations of adventurers, and each one takes away a special feeling from the spectacular Lundbreck Falls. The Falls are 7.5 metres high and have long been a favourite spot for both amateur and more serious fishing. If you arrive early in the morning or early in the evening, Lundbreck Falls will provide you with one of its beautiful rainbows.

Lundbreck Area

The little hamlet of Lundbreck enjoys one of the most sublime settings in Alberta high on a rolling plateau at the dividing point between prairie and foothill. The opening in the Rocky Mountains, ahead, is the entrance to the Crowsnest Pass. On a clear day, you can see Turtle Mountain.

The white scar left by the gigantic Frank Slide of 1903 is visible even at this distance.

Like other ranges in Southern Alberta, these mountains, consisting of sedimentary rocks laid down millennia ago on the floor of an ancient sea, have been pushed slowly eastward along low-angle thrust faults. This gigantic shifting in the earth's crust accounts for some of the rocky outcrops visible on either side of the highway west of Lundbreck.

Valley glaciers combined with water erosion and steady west winds have shaped this landscape over thousands of years. The terraced valley sides were created when the valley was blocked by the Laurentide Ice sheet during the last glacial epoch.

The Crowsnest River is one of the most celebrated trout streams in North America, but still yielding superb rainbow trout. Many fishermen visiting here support the catch-and-release style of fishing.

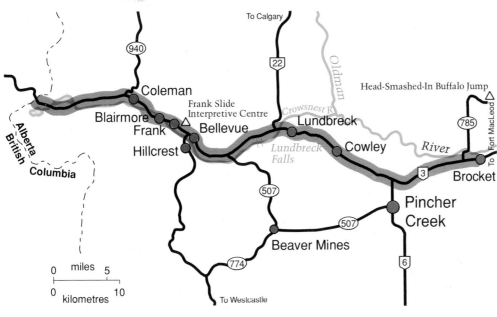

In the Pass

Leitch Collieries Historic Site

This Provincial Historic Site, located in a grassy valley known as Police Flats just a few kilometres west of Lundbreck Falls, allows you a chance to explore the ruins of an authentic turn-of-the-century coal mine. Leitch Collieries, which was financed by Canadians, was forced to shut down in 1915 because of dropping coal prices. Displays and guided summer tours of the

Leitch Collieries opened in 1907 with two mines. By 1910, over one hundred coal ovens had been built at Police Flats.

mine site provide an exciting introduction to the mining history of the Crowsnest Pass.

Burmis

Burmis was once the site of a major coal mine and railroad marshalling yard. The treed slopes you see here and in the Pass proper were once wide grassy meadows, home to prehistoric bison and horses. Fish and game were abundant, and the Chinook wind, then as now, helped to keep the ranges open for grazing of game animals.

Archaeologists have estimated that in the past 10,000 years, some 500 generations of prehistoric peoples frequented the Crowsnest Pass. More than 250 prehistoric sites have been found here. Not surprisingly, the ancient people pitched their tents in the same locations that the newcomers built their towns, where fuel, water and protection from the wind were close at hand.

Coal Country

Among the sedimentary rocks that make up these mountains are those of the Kootenay formation, crucial to the economic history of the Pass. This formation contains massive coal seams that began as plantlife in ancient swamps during the age of the dinosaur. Mountain building produced pro-

The early coal mines of the Crowsnest Pass usually had two shafts - one for entry and the other for ventilation.

found compressive forces that changed the organic material into coal, and at the same time, the layers of rock here were slowly folded into synclines and anticlines.

In 1882, G.W. Dawson of the Geological Survey made an assessment of the coal fields and timber potential in the Pass. Mining and logging promised rich rewards for the Canadian Pacific Railway's freighting business. The railroad would have been first built through the Crowsnest Pass rather than the Bow River Gap had it not been for its proximity to the U.S. border, raising the risk of easy American access to Canadian territory.

However, with the main line completed, the CPR sought to provide Canadian access to Crowsnest and

Southern British Columbia coal and mining resources. Surveys on the Crowsnest line were completed in 1892 and the railroad was finished just six years later.

Over the years from 1901 to 1957, more than ten different coal mines worked in the Pass. Immigrants, many with mining experience in the old country, converged on the area, Czechs, Poles, Austri-ans and Italians rubbing shoulders with English, Belgian and Scottish miners. Small communities emerged in close proximity to the mines, since it was not practical to transport miners long distances over poor roads and trails. Some of these communities are little more than memories, but five of them still survive along Highway 3 within the Municipality of Crowsnest Pass.

Bellevue

Bellevue, established in 1901, is a picturesque mountain town. "Quelle belle vue!" cried a young lady gazing on the site for the first time back in 1903, and "Bellevue" it remains today. Gazing up at a few miners' cottages precariously perched near a cliff, you may notice an old mine portal protected now with rusty iron bars. A stream of clear water pours out from its dark mouth, sparkling in the sunlight.

In the Bellevue Cafe in 1920, Constable Bailey of the Alberta Provincial Police and Constable Usher of the Royal Canadian Mounted Police were killed in a shootout with two train robbers, part of a bizarre trio named Arloff, Bassoff and Arkoff. The police killed Arkoff on the spot, but Bassoff escaped. He was eventually captured and executed, while Arloff would later die in jail.

Hillcrest

Just south of Bellevue lies Hillcrest, a hamlet spread among the pines and aspens below Turtle Mountain. This idyllic little settlement rates an entry in *The Canadian Encyclopedia* for a tragic reason. Here, on June 19, 1914, the worst mine disaster in Canada occurred when a gas explosion caused the death of 189 miners. Those who were not killed outright were found head down near pools of water, where they had made futile attempts to escape. Two mass graves in the nearby cemetery remain as mute memorials to the tragedy.

Turtle Mountain and the Frank Slide serve as grim reminders of the dangers faced by turn-of-the-century inhabitants of the Crowsnest Pass.

The Frank Slide

The picturesque Pass communities are no strangers to such tragedies. Just outside Bellevue is the location of the Frank Slide, one of the largest landslides in recorded history. The Indians knew Turtle Mountain as "The Mountain That Walks." When it took a tiny step at 4:10 A.M. on April 29, 1903, a gigantic wedge of limestone, some 30 million cubic metres, crashed down on part of the town of Frank. In 100 seconds, it destroyed a mine entrance and part of the town, covered the railway with a wall of rock, and claimed 70 lives.

At the edge of the Slide, by Gold Creek, a paved road winds up to the Frank Slide Interpretive Centre, a modern facility offering an awe-inspiring view of the Slide. Here, you can learn the whole story of the disaster, and much more about the coal mining history of the Pass. It is a story of tragedy and of gallant heroism by mine rescue teams, but it is also one of hope and, at times, of ribald humour. The Centre offers photographic displays, audio-visual programmes, interpretive talks, and an interesting shop for visitor purchases.

As you pass the west end of modern-day Frank, a tumbledown building on the south side of the tracks marks a sulphur spring which was once thought to be of great medicinal value. There is a small trail to the springs, where wild ducks and geese are often found feeding in a nearby lagoon.

The people of the Pass and their colorful history are brought to life through displays, pictures and interpretive programs.

Blairmore

It's not uncommon to see a herd of bighorn sheep at the east edge of Blairmore, the business centre of the Pass. Muledeer and elk frequent the nearby valleys, as do black bear and an occasional grizzly. Not surprisingly, the Pass has long been popular with hunters and fishermen. In more recent times, the area has begun to celebrate the opportunities for cross-country skiing at nearby Allison Lake, and for horseback riding, hiking and mountaineering in the

The Frank Slide Interpretive Centre sits in the shadow of Turtle Mountain.

surrounding valleys. The combination of colourful mining towns and high alpine scenery draws photographers and visual artists. Blairmore has developed a ski hill on the south side of town, and a 9-hole golf course next to Highway 3. There are a number of historic residences and public buildings that make a drive down the side streets a detour to discovery. Visitor information is available.

The Crowsnest Ecomuseum

Pass people are proud of their eventful history, and their cosmopolitan cultural mix. That pride has led them to welcome the founding of an Ecomuseum, encompassing the corridor from Burmis to

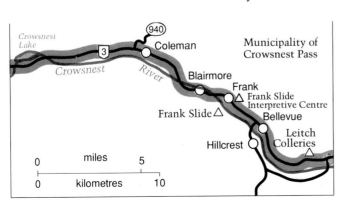

Crowsnest Lake. This is not a museum in the usual sense: the roof is not man-made; it is the sky itself. The Ecomuseum includes not only the coal mining exhibits presently in place, but also clusters of unique buildings, wildlife habitats, and the cultures and traditions of the people of Crowsnest. The Ecomuseum plans include, among other things, tours of coal mines and tours to view the "boom town" architectural motifs of Hillcrest, Bellevue and Coleman. It will also celebrate the music and oral history of the pass, and take visitors on walking tours of the surrounding landscape to view the rich flora and fauna.

Coleman

Below Highway 3, among the red roofs of Coleman, the Crowsnest Museum gives some insight into the rugged lives and dangerous conditions the early generations endured to keep the fires of industry burning. Next to the museum, a scenic miner's path allows you to walk in the footsteps of the early miners. Stop at the picnic tables and listen to the waters of the Nez Perce Creek, or bring your tennis racquet for the nearby tennis courts.

The moose is the largest member of the deer family. To spot a moose, look towards brush and water rather than thick forest.

Beavers have tiny legs, large tails and big teeth. The beavers' teeth never stop growing and therefore they must continually gnaw to keep their teeth at a workable length.

Rum Runners

The prohibition era was a colourful and exciting time. The majority of Albertans voted for prohibition in 1915, but coal mining is a thirst-provoking activity, and it wasn't surprising that the Pass voted over-whelmingly "wet."

Canoeing on the Crowsnest River

At first the drinkers got their wares by simply ordering supplies from out-of-province sources, through the Dominion Express office. In 1921, that source dried up and the moonshiners and bootleggers came to the forefront. Despite the efforts of the Alberta Provincial Police to stamp out the trade, booze flowed into the Pass via pack horse, dog-team and most notoriously, the McLaughlin Buick, or Whiskey Six. One of the most enterprising smugglers stashed his whiskey in rubber bags inside hog carcasses bound for market.

At the centre of the smuggling trade was Emilio Picariello, or "Emperor Pic," a local entrepreneur and prohibition-era Robin Hood. He was well loved throughout the Pass for his generosity to the poor, and affection for him lingers on, even though the life of the portly Emperor ended on the gallows. Pic and a female associate, convicted in the shooting of a police-man, were both hanged in 1923.

Towards Crowsnest

Just west of Coleman, the highway passes through a rock cut from one of the few igneous volcanic intrusions in Alberta. Great excitement was caused recently when a prospector rediscovered gold here.

West of Coleman, Crowsnest Mountain trans-fixes the viewer, with the High Rock Range visible to the north and the Flathead Range to the south. Now the valley opens up, with the Crowsnest River looping in blue below the highway. Ahead lies the turn-off to Allison Lake. There is a beautiful camp-ground located here, and a trout hatchery on Allison Creek offers tours and self-guided walks. In winter, the same area provides some of the most exciting groomed cross-country trails in Alberta.

Highway 3 continues

through a wide, scenic valley. The tiny village of Sentinel sits close to the shores of Crowsnest Lake. The lake is an inviting picnic spot on a sunny day, and despite the temperature of the water, you may see wet-suited sail-boarders skimming across the windswept waters. Bighorn sheep are seen frequently in the area, often coming down to the road. On the lakeshore is a significant archaeological site, with artifacts dating back up to 8,000 years.

Crowsnest Mountain near the Alberta - B.C. border

The Summit of the Pass

Near the summit of the Pass, the road crosses Island Lake, where high cliffs dip into the deep, chilly waters. In the winter, you may see the tiny shacks of ice fishermen out on the windswept lake. A few kilometres further on, below the road, is the tiny hamlet of Crowsnest, straddling the Alberta-B.C. border.

Now the rivers change direction as we cross the Great Divide. Ahead lie the communities of Natal, Michel and Fernie, with their own stories to tell, ones that are not limited by mere provincial borders. These towns share ties of blood and iron with Hillcrest, Bellevue, Frank, Blairmore and Coleman, the flamboyant Pass communities of Alberta.

The Ranchlands Tour

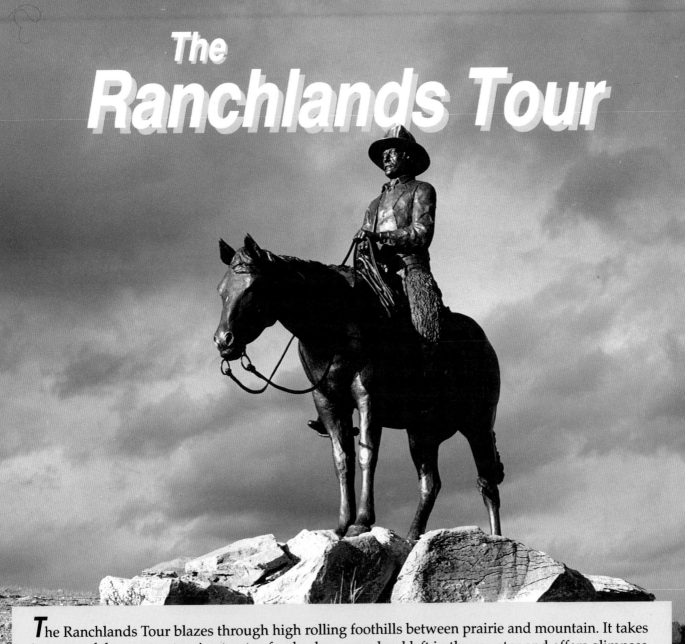

*T*he Ranchlands Tour blazes through high rolling foothills between prairie and mountain. It takes in some of the most extensive tracts of unbroken rangeland left in the country and offers glimpses of a culture on which the West was built. This is ranching country.

In the late 1800s, the buffalo all but wiped out and the native people moved to reservations, the foothills and high plains spread, uninhabited, like an open invitation. Thousands of beating hooves sounded in the distance and cowboys hooted and whistled, as they drove cattle north from Idaho, Wyoming and Montana. A new railroad linked the West with international markets, territorial conflicts with the Indian people were over, and the Canadian government was leasing land in the foothills area at a cent an acre annually — for tracts of up to 40,000 hectares (100,000 acres).

With the cattle came a unique kind of man, one who loved the wide-open spaces and endured all measure of hardship for a lifestyle he felt was free. Eastern Canadian businessmen invested in the land, as did British aristocrats and American citizens.

The lawlessness which prevailed south of the border was not tolerated in the Canadian West. Shootouts and brawls were rare, and the ranchers' entertainment was fox hunts, horse races, polo events, and grand Christmas balls. Although many homes were built of logs, the interiors often contained small libraries of imported books, fine furnishings, china and a piano or organ.

Cochrane and South

The tour begins at the town of Cochrane, a close-knit farm and ranch community.

The history of ranching is remembered at Cochrane Ranche Site, a 375-hectare park on the west side of the town. On a wind-swept hilltop, larger than life, a bronze of horse and rider watches over the sweeping rangeland where Alberta's cattle industry began. The "Men of Vision" monument is a memorial to the many pioneers of the ranching industry, including Senator Matthew Cochrane.

In 1881, Cochrane leased 40,000 hectares (100,000 acres) along the Bow River, purchased 12,000 cattle in Montana and Wyoming and then had them herded north to an area near what is now Cochrane. It was Canada's first large-scale leasehold operation. In 1882 and 1883, however, severe winter weather killed one third of the Cochrane Ranche herd and the remaining cattle were moved south, near Fort Macleod. The operation in the south profited, and in 1885 was part of the largest round-up in Canadian history with 100 cowboys gathering 60,000 cattle between Pincher Creek and Nanton.

Bragg Creek

Follow Highway 22 as it winds through the forest to the hamlet of Bragg Creek. The air is spiced with the tang of spruce and the smoke from wood-burning fireplaces. No wonder the area is the inspiration for so many talented artists and craftspeople, whose work can be seen at shops and galleries throughout Bragg Creek. From the hamlet, follow the clean, cold water of the Elbow River upstream about a kilometre to Bragg Creek Provincial Park and enjoy the large, open picnic area and secluded trails. This attractive area was chosen as the site of North America's first hostel, in 1953. Farther west along Highway 66 is Elbow Falls, which offers opportunities for fishing, hiking, horseback riding and off-road vehicle use.

Millarville

On a summer day in 1905, settlers from the region gathered enthusiastically at Millarville for one of Alberta's first horse races. By 1941, the tiny community was hosting the 13th largest horse race in Canada. Provincial-level races are still held each summer at the track, which is west of town on Highway 762, and the site is also used for annual craft sales, agricultural fairs and summer Saturday markets.

Farther west in the wind-tousled hills, the Leighton Arts Centre provides inspirational settings for potters, weavers, sculptors and painters. There are galleries, displays and a craft shop in the unique home of two artists: the late A.C. and Barbara Leighton.

On Highway 22 at Millarville, an old general store serves farmers and ranchers, as it has since 1926.

Turner Valley

Originally leased as ranchland, Turner Valley made Canadian history in 1914, when the country's first major crude oil discovery was made. Present in great quantities with the oil, natural gas

A typical cattle drive in Alberta's foothills

Interpretive centre at Cochrane Ranch

Cochrane

1A

Bow

Calgary

1

Bragg Creek

22X

Priddis

River

Millarville

Okotoks

Turner Valley

Black Diamond

High River

541

Longview

R

22

Highwood

To Kananaskis

Nanton

533

Chain Lakes Prov. Park

Porcupine

520

Hills

Claresholm

2

Oldman

Head – Smashed – In Buffalo Jump

River

Crowsnest

785

Pass

Lundbreck

3

Fort MacLeod

0   miles   10

0   kilometres   20

Pincher Creek

seeps from cracks in the ground. During the oil boom, the gas was burned off and the roar from "Hell's Half Acre," the location of the many gas flares, was loud enough to be heard in Calgary. Today, the flares are gone, but in some places at Hell's Half Acre the seepages still burn.

The Tourist Information Centre located under the oil derrick on Main Street has a number of publications on the area.

Black Diamond

Built on the banks of the Sheep River, the town of Black Diamond was named for the coal once mined here. The Sheep is a gentle river, perfect for drifting lazily along on an inner tube or in a dingy. You can float for miles, but bring along a support vehicle because it can be a long walk back.

On the first weekend in June, Black Diamond Ranch plays host to a Canadian Professional Rodeo, kicked off by a parade through town.

The Big Rock

During the most recent ice age, the side of a mountain in what is now Jasper National Park tumbled onto the surface of a glacier and moved south. When the glacier melted, it left about 2000 quartzite blocks called

Ranching in the Porcupine Hills is assisted by the Chinook winds which make it possible for cattle to graze year-round.

"erratics" in its wake. The largest is the Big Rock, halfway between Black Diamond and Okotoks on Highway 7, which has been declared a provincial historic site.

Longview

Rarely is a town as appropriately named as Longview. It was born during the oil boom and was optimistically named "Little New York," but the boom was short-lived, and the permanent residents, ranchers and farmers, renamed their town to express the feeling of spaciousness which they loved. Here, there is indeed a long view: west to the mountains and east to the prairies.

Porcupine Hills

" . . . we rode to the top of Porcupine Hill and from there and the south end of the spur, had I think, one of the most magnificent views I ever saw in my life. At a distance varying from 24 to 30 kilometres, in a sort of immense amphitheatre lay the Rocky Mountains towering their giant heads many thousand feet high, on our left the boundless prairie stretching far to the Eastward . . ." (Colonel Patrick Robertson-Ross, 1872)

The gentle, rounded Porcupine Hills east of Highway 22 lie between mountains and plain, yet belong to neither. Although geographically part of the foothills, the Porcupine Hills are geologically unique, for the gently dipping bedrock is characteristic of the plains. The Peigan Indians called the formation Porcupine Trail, because the tapering silhouettes of the hills bristled, like quills, with Douglas fir and limber pine.

Ranches with a Past

Many of the ranches described here are day guest ranches as well as bed and breakfast ranches. It is important to check with local tourism information centres regarding availability, times, seasons, and telephone numbers.

Bar U Ranch

Many cowboys, including the infamous Sundance Kid, rode for the Bar U Ranch: one of the first and largest ranches in the area. At one time, the Bar U ran 30,000 cattle. The original ranch buildings, scattered on either side of Pekisco Creek, give the ranch the appearance of a small village.

The Alberta Rose

EP Ranch and Teahouse

In 1919, Edward Prince of Wales was shopping for ranchland in southwestern Alberta. Interested in the area's potential, he had hoped to improve stock-breeding there. West of the Bar U Ranch, he purchased 10,000 hectares (the equivalent of about six square miles) of prime grazing land and named it EP (Edward Prince). He visited the ranch several times,

The Big Rock near Okotoks

once with his new wife, Wallis Simpson, the woman for whom he had abdicated the throne. The main residence, built in 1923, is today a quiet tearoom with memorabilia of British royalty.

Chain Lakes Provincial Park

Just west of the highway, Chain Lakes is a perfect place to stop for a picnic lunch, overnight camping or just a refreshing dip in

Long-horned cattle near Longview

the reservoir lake. Chain Lakes is stocked with rainbow trout which provide sport for the adult angler, and there is also a trout fishing pond for the children. In the winter it is a very popular location for ice fishing.

A7 Ranch Lookout

A. E. Cross was a consummate businessman who started as a veterinarian in Montreal. After he'd moved west, Cross established one of Alberta's largest ranches and a successful Calgary brewing company. He was one of the four cattlemen who financed the first Calgary Stampede in 1912. An interpretive sign along

Highway 533 overlooks the original Cross holdings; although the A7 has been divided into smaller units, it still remains in the Cross family.

Percival Ranch

The Two Dot Ranch was established in 1884, running up to 15,000 longhorn cattle on a 17,600 hectare lease. In 1959, Frederick Percival, the Earl of Egmont, purchased the Two Dot and moved with his family from England, proving that the lure of the West has not abated. Today the area has been established as a game preserve.

Nanton

Turn east and follow Highway 533 to Nanton where some of Canada's finest drinking water is bottled by the Nanton Spring Water Company which markets carbonated and flavoured water throughout the world.

Another attraction at Nanton is the Lancaster Bomber. This plane is one of the 430 Lancasters manufactured in Canada. It was flown to England in 1945 but arrived too late to see any action. After the war, it was used for reconnaissance purposes. In 1958, a group of Nanton businessmen purchased the aircraft and transported it to Nanton to be put on display. It is the most valuable vintage aircraft west of Ontario.

Return to Chain Lakes Provincial Park via Highway 533, or continue south on Highway 2.

Guest ranch in the foothills

Oxley Ranch and the Leavings

In 1881, the area's first homesteader, Henry Kountz, sold his land to a large ranching company owned in part by English MP Alexander Stavely-Hill. A log cabin was built on the south side of the property and used by the North West Mounted Police and travellers as a stopover between Fort Macleod and Calgary. It was named "The Leavings" to remind travellers that they were leaving the last supply of wood and water before Calgary. The cistern at the old cabin is

still in use by its present owners as their water reservoir. The sandstone barn, with its specially treated tree trunk floorboards, and wooden hayloft top built with square nails, is also still in use. The building and ranch settings along Willow Creek are unique and one can readily visualize the police and other travellers coming to this welcoming stopover location.

Claresholm

In 1902, Clare Amundsen unpacked the few possessions she had taken on her journey from North Dakota with her husband and 23 other farmers. For the rest of her life, this would be Clare's home: and this is how the town got its name. Some of the pioneers' original belongings are displayed at the Claresholm Museum.

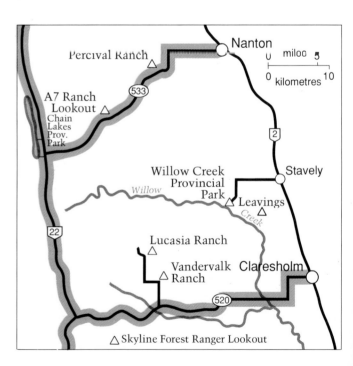

Historical Museum at Claresholm

During World War II, Canada was the aircrew training centre for the British Empire and allies. Eight flight schools were established in Southern Alberta, including one in Claresholm.

Claresholm remains a busy flight base. It has hosted national and international gliding, soaring, and parachuting competitions. A Canadian sailplane soaring record of 803 kilometres was accomplished from Claresholm in 1982. Strong westerly winds called chinooks allow for glider flights to altitudes of 9,000 metres.

This town is also known for its National Appaloosa Horse Club of Canada Museum. It houses photos of this famous spotted breed of horse, as well as saddles, clothing and national horse show trophies from past competitions.

Return to ranching country down Highway 520 to the junction with Highway 22.

Vandervalk Ranch

Vandervalk Ranch was started in 1882 by three railroad men and many of their original buildings are still standing. The operation, originally called the Glengarry Ranching Company, was expanded too quickly and didn't prosper until cattle baron Pat Burns purchased its 960 hectares for his famous 44 Ranch. Today, the Vandervalks raise and sell valuable cattle and bulls.

Lucasia Ranch

In 1881, Captain C. A. Lyndon started a cattle ranch here, but today the emphasis has shifted to prize-winning appaloosa and percheron horses. Percheron stallions imported from England and France are used to produce fine offspring sold around

the world as show and work horses. Visitors are welcome to view the operation.

Skyline Forest Ranger Lookout Tower

As you travel west on Highway 520, you move ever upward into the Porcupine Hills. At the crest of the hills, turn south and drive up to the Skyline Forest Ranger Lookout Tower, on of the highest points in the hills. As you gaze over this land of gentle slopes, ridges and valleys, you'll be able to see how the Porcupine Hills link the Livingstone Ranges of Rockies in the west with the Alberta Ranchlands sprawling to the east. You may also notice wildlife such as wild turkeys, elk, white-tailed and mule deer, pheasants and the sharp-tailed grouse.

Oldman River

Turning south on Highway 22, you'll soon cross the Oldman River. Indian people called this Napi's River. Napi means the Old One. The Oldman River tumbles down from the Rockies in a long stretch of cold, clear water. Fishing is good, and camping is available a few kilometres south at Lundbreck Falls.

This original log house, built in the 1880s, is now part of the Vandervalk Ranch. The countryside is dotted by remnants of the past such as this wagon near the Lucasia Ranch.

Western Dress

The working clothes of modern western Canadian cowboys owe much to history and more to practicality. The wide-brimmed felt hat shades the eyes from the glaring sun and protects the back of the neck from the cold November sleet. The bandanna, when pulled over the nose and mouth, enables riders to breathe even in the dust raised by a herd of 10,000 cattle. The heels of the boots keep feet securely in the stirrups, over endless miles at round-up time.

Comfort, and durability are the characteristics of western wear. Stores which cater to western dress are found in most towns along the Ranchlands Tour.

When you dress Western, you are touching Alberta's past.

Branding in the Porcupine Hills - a practice dating back 150 years.

Acknowledgements

Financial Sponsors

Canada / Alberta Tourism Agreement - Panorama Public and Industrial Communications Ltd. (Calgary)

Management Committee / Project Sponsors

Phil Robart (Chair), Calgary Tourist and Convention Bureau (Hap Freeman, Original Member)
Yvonne Fisher, Big Country Tourist Association
Glenda Leitch, South East Alberta Travel and Convention Association
Beth Russell, Chinook Country Tourist Association (Al Bailey, Original Member)

Advisors

Alberta Culture and Multiculturalism, Alberta Recreation and Parks, Travel Alberta.

Production

Project Management: Art New, Panorama Public and Industrial Communications Ltd.
Editor: Mary Walters Riskin, Lone Pine Publishing
Design: Yuet Chan
Graphics: Yuet Chan, Ewa Pluciennik
Mapping: Don Inman (Central Map), Rick Checkland (Route Maps)
Writers: Fred Stenson, Sid Marty, Lee Christie
Contributing Writer: David McIntyre
Photographers:

 Major Contributors: Doug Leighton, Scott Rowed, Egon Bork, Ellis Anderson, Derrek Boddington, Mach 2 Stock Exchange, Take Stock Inc.

 Other Contributors: Cameron Young, Sam Albert, Eastern Irrigation District, City of Calgary, City of Medicine Hat, City of Lethbridge, Glenbow Museum, Mel Halverson, Simonne Flynn, John Walper, Rob Enns, Mel Buschert, Mike Drew, Cliff Cates, Ted Dawson, Cliff Wallace, David McIntyre, Geological Survey of Canada, Panorama Public and Industrial Communications Ltd., and special thanks to Travel Alberta and Alberta Culture and Multiculturalism

Advisors to Panorama: Bill Ashton, Friesen Design Associates, Lone Pine Publishing Ltd.
Printing: Commercial Colour Press Ltd.

Community Advisory Committees

The Historic Crowsnest Corridor: Cliff Reiling, David McIntyre, Brad Lucas, Helen Termaine
Waterton Lakes Heritage Tour: Brian Baker, Howard Snyder, Beth Russell, Charles Zinkan
Market Garden Tour: Shelby MacLeod, Murray Coleman, Ray Evanson, Lynn Wenbourne, Earl Ellington, Dale Clifton
The Kananaskis Tour: Elaine Mason, Bill Thompson, Reed Purnell, Glenda Cutforth, Jackie Chang, Margaret Fraser
The Ranchlands Tour: Mae Weber, June Melvin, Reed Purnell, Mary Buckley
The Red Coat Trail: Lyle Nattrass, Louise Heric, Roy Hummell, Jean Swihart, Randy Smith
Calgary: Janice Cullen, Phil Robart and other members of the Calgary Tourist and Convention Bureau
The Kinbrook Tour: Sandra Walliser, Frank Chute, Jim Webber, John Walper
The Buffalo Trail: Fred Ammann, Don White, Ron Davis, Keith Bocking, Glenda Leitch
The Dinosaur Tour: Bill Martynes, Yvonne Fisher

HOW TO

Ten Perfect

In Southern

EDMONTON 2

TROCHU 585

27 27 21 56

22

940

9

COCHRANE 1A 21

CANMORE

KANANASKIS TOUR

40

1

CALGARY

2 9 840

STRATHMORE

56

DINOSAUR TOUR

CALGARY

1

SPRUCE MEADOWS

22X

BASSANO

DINOSAUR PROVINCIAL PARK

BROOKS

KINBROOK TOUR

36

1

BUFFALO TRAIL

Alberta

523

885

MEDICINE HAT

3

BOW ISLAND

41

TABER

3

MARKET GARDEN TOUR

4

61

FOREMOST

RED COAT TRAIL

CYPRESS HILLS PROVINCIAL PARK

4

879

Alberta

MILK RIVER

501

WILD HORSE

COUTTS

232

A.

PANORAMA
COMMUNICATIONS
CALGARY

15

Stamp Around Alberta

Have one stamp on each route stamped at a Travel Information Centre and receive a 10% discount on your next purchase of *Ten Perfect Vacations*. Obtain 25 stamps and receive a 20% discount. Send page to Panorama Communications. (Address: inside front cover)

The Kananaskis Tour

- High River
- Peter Lougheed Information Centre
- Canmore

Calgary

- Burns Building, 237 - 8 Ave. S.E.
- West Booth Canada Olympic Park
- East Booth 6220 - 16 Ave. N.E.
- Calgary International Airport Arrivals Level, Main Terminal
- Calgary International Airport South Booth (June 3 - Sept. 4)

The Dinosaur Tour

- Brooks
- S.E. Entrance, Drumheller
- N.E. Entrance, Drumheller
- Hanna
- Trochu

The Kinbrook Tour

- Brooks

The Buffalo Trail

- Medicine Hat
- Walsh
- Oyen

The Red Coat Trail

- Travel Alberta Milk River
- 2805 Scenic Drive Lethbridge
- Brewery Hill Lethbridge
- Fort Macleod
- Travel Alberta Fort Mcleod
- Head-Smashed-In Buffalo Jump

Market Garden Tour

- Taber
- Bow Island

Waterton Lakes Heritage Tour

- Pincher Creek
- Entrance to Waterton Townsite

- Tamarack Mall Waterton Townsite
- Cardston
- Mountain View

The Historic Crowsnest Corridor

- Frank Slide Interpretive Centre
- Frank Slide Chamber of Commerce
- Travel Alberta Sentinal

The Ranchlands Tour

- Cochrane
- Turner Valley
- Okotoks
- Nanton
- Claresholm